Portrait of Wildlife on a Hill Farm

PORTRAIT OF

ANNE McBRIDE AND TONY PEARCE

with a Foreword by PROF. DAVID BELLAMY

PAINTINGS BY DARREN REES

WILDLIFE ON A
HILL FARM

Whittet Books

Title page illustration: VIEW OF GILFACH FARM FROM THE OAKWOOD.

First published 1995
Text © 1995 by Anne McBride and Tony Pearce
Illustrations ©1995 by Darren Rees
Whittet Books Ltd, 18 Anley Road, London W14 OBY

Design by Paul Minns

ISBN 1 873580 18 5

British Library Cataloguing in Publication Data. A catalogue record for this book
is available from the British Library.

Printed in Hong Kong by Midas

CONTENTS

Map of Gilfach Farm   6/7

Acknowledgments   8

Foreword by David Bellamy   9

1 The Rocks beneath our Feet   11

2 Homes for Men and Animals   30

3 Hanging Oaks   55

4 Timber!   87

5 Life in the Fast Lane   101

6 Wild Hills and Friendly Fields 123

7 Here Today, Gone Tomorrow   152

Index   157

Old Railway

Gilfach

Tunnel

N
W E
S

ACKNOWLEDGMENTS

First, my apologies to all those who have helped with this book and who, because of bad memory and lack of space, I have not named. Nonetheless, please accept my thanks. To name but a few: to Trevor Williams, Kevin Roberts, Mike Pratt and Paul Beech for their specialist knowledge and to Jenny Limond for making sure it all made sense to the non-expert. To Frank Lancaster, a well known figure tramping across Gilfach on his fungus forays. To Dave Hargreaves, conservation officer of the Radnorshire Wildlife Trust. To my friends in mid-Wales who have deepened my love of their country. To my friends in England for their humour and moral support, especially my colleagues at the Anthrozoology Institute. To my father for casting his critical eye over my, often idiosyncratic, use of the English language. To Annabel Whittet for her patience. To Darren Rees for enhancing the text with his illustrations. To Tony Pearce without whose hard work in helping with the research (and excellent coffee-making and pizza-purchasing skills), this book would not have come to fruition. For this he has truly earned co-authorship. For my part, I take full responsibility for the text and trust that it lives up to all their, and your expectations.

This book was completed in the year of my parent's golden wedding anniversary and I would like to dedicate it to them and all those in my life who have shown me that happiness comes to the person who

finds tongues in trees, books in the running brooks,
Sermons in stones, and good in everything

As You Like It

ANNE McBRIDE

Gilfach OS ref SN965717

FOREWORD

BY PROF. DAVID BELLAMY

Once upon a time, thanks to the Mid-Wales Festival of the Countryside, I had the opportunity of flying over the Magical Kingdom in a helicopter. The hilltops were covered with misty clouds, so we had to nose our way up the valleys to find our way through to the coast.

There below me was the greenest landscape I have ever seen. An ordered jumble of small fields, all set about with hedgerows, dry stone walls, lanes and trackways which meandered about as if they too were seeking their way over the misty hills.

All was people made and people managed, carved out of the Cambrian Forests eons ago and kept in good green heart by the hands-on wisdom of farming families. Nature in all her diverse glory was still there, not subdued, but enhanced by the continuity of family life.

The whole sang the song of wise use, *Cynefin y Cymro*, the land of all our yesterdays, the hope for all our tomorrows.

I wanted to gather it all up, the healing essence of Wales, and take it home.

Now, thanks to this wonderful book, I can do just that, thanks to the knowledge, talent and devotion of the authors and the artist.

Bedburn, October 1994

———

THE ROCKS BENEATH
OUR FEET

Gilfach is a small valley in mid-Wales, near Rhayader, caught, by a combination of location and fate, in a time warp. A time warp which has bequeathed it beauty and peace in which we can enjoy the natural gifts we once had in abundance. Gilfach ranges in elevation from 240 to 460 metres (788 to 1,509 feet) and faces predominantly towards the north. It is a small site, a mere 413 acres (167 hectares), but its importance lies in the fact that it contains a rich variety of habitats. A patchwork of miniature pastures, bounded by hedgerows and stone walls, leads one's eyes down to the River Marteg; here a babbling brook, there a tumbling torrent. Also winding its way through the valley is an abandoned railway line. The metallic clackety-clack of wheels has been replaced by the silent flitting of bats, for the railway tunnel is ideal for bats in winter.

Surrounding the valley are the stark, open moorlands of the Cambrian mountains, crouched like protective lions with manes of oakwood and conifer plantation. Tucked in the paws of the furthest hill are the farm buildings, an 18th-century barn and a 16th-century longhouse. Though a family farm for over 200 years, the site was virtually abandoned from 1965 until 1988, when its conservation potential was fully appreciated and it was bought by the then recently formed Radnorshire Wildlife Trust.

Gilfach lies at the meeting point of the River Wye and one of its tributaries, the Marteg. For many decades, it has been a favourite haunt for birdwatchers, picnickers and walkers. Whilst those who visit Gilfach are struck by the serenity of the scenery, I suspect most give little thought as to how it all came about. The rocks of Gilfach form the basis of all we see around us — the leonine hills, the murmuring Marteg, the soils and even the local climate. In turn, they influence which species of flower can grow, the variety of wildlife that can inhabit the valley and finally the form of agriculture that man can practise.

We need to indulge our imaginations as we trace the history of these rocks from their beginnings, millions of years ago, at the bottom of the sea, to their being pushed upwards by the momentous forces of the earth's crust, to form high, craggy mountains.

The rocks underlying Gilfach, and protruding as the cliffs and outcrops of Wyloer Hill, are known as Tarannon and Llandovery shales. These were laid down

Previous page illustration: VIEW FROM GILFACH UP MARCHEINI VALLEY.

———

under a primeval sea as layers of mud and clay. Welded by the pressure of the water and weight of ever more sediment deposited from above, they were formed into thin layers of rock, the shales. The word 'shale' originates from the Old English word for shell or scale, which accurately describes the bedded rock. The shales took many millions of years to form and these rocks date back to the Ordovician period which began some 475 million years ago, lasting some 30 million years. This was followed by the Silurian period, during which more rock layers were laid down. These, and younger rock layers have been worn away and are no longer visible at Gilfach. The Silurian age lasted about 40 million years ending 400 million years ago, give or take the odd million or two!

Much early geology, including the names of geological epochs used as standards around the world, was the work of one Roderick Murchison. Murchison did field studies in Wales in the mid-1800s. Indeed, he named both the Ordovician and Silurian periods after two ancient Celtic tribes, the Ordovices and the Silures. From prehistoric times, the Silures lived in the area surrounding the upper reaches of the Rivers Wye, Usk and Severn. In AD43 the second Roman invasion, that of Emperor Claudius, began. The Silures, along with other Welsh tribes, were temporarily brought together under the famous Caractacus. With his leadership they waged an indomitable resistance, fighting a guerrilla war against the professional Roman army. They managed to hold the enemy off from penetrating the Welsh borders for six years until AD50. Then, like many settled regions between the Rivers Wash and Severn, they too were defeated and became part of the Roman domain. The Romans did bring trade and an era of relative peace to the country, though neither they, nor later invaders ever truly conquered more than the borderland of Wales. Thus, the heritage of the Silures and Ordovices are passed down in the Celtic traditions of the modern Welsh and in their language which, before the Romans, was the common tongue of much of Britain.

Their namesakes, the Ordovician and Silurian rocks, often yield a variety of fossils, but please remember these should not be collected from the reserve. The most common fossil type of the Ordovician rocks are those of small, almost flat, fretsaw-shaped remains called graptolites. These fossils are the calcium structures in which communities of tiny creatures, called 'polyps', lived. These polyps lived in miniature coral-like structures. Unlike modern corals which are attached to solid surfaces, some species of graptolite were free-floating throughout their lives. From the later Silurian period, the most commonly found fossils are those of

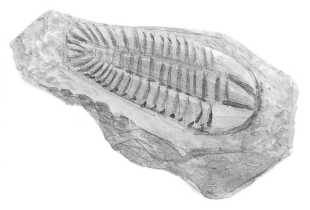

A TRILOBITE.

primitive crustacea called trilobites, who are distant relatives of animals such as crabs and lobsters. Trilobites were bottom dwellers, earning their living by digging about in the muddy seabed. They were the dominant life form in these early seas for many millions of years. Indeed some species have been found to have had a worldwide distribution. However, their watery rule ended with the conclusion of the Silurian period.

The Silurian period was followed by that of the Devonian, a time of massive landscape changes. In brief, it was now that the mountains of Wales, amongst others, were pushed up from the sea as the plates of the earth's crust moved closer together. On two of these plates sit the continents of Europe and America, and as these plates moved towards each other they squashed up the sediments forming the floor of the Atlantic Ocean. All this movement was accompanied by dramatic volcanic eruptions and earthquakes. Such events may be visually dramatic, but they are soon over. The mountains then formed were not rounded, rather they were jagged and craggy like the Alps and Himalayas. The peaked shapes we associate with ranges such as the Andes and Rockies today are characteristic of young, newly formed mountains. For some 400 million years, after the Devonian upheavals, wind and rain weathered and subdued the older, Welsh mountain tops, aided to a large extent by the glaciers of the succeeding Ice Ages.

In Britain's relatively warm modern climate, rain will fall as rain in the summer and as snow in the winter up to about 2,000 metres (6,564 feet) above sea level, that is about twice the height of Snowdon (Snowdon's peak is 1,085 metres / 3, 560 feet above sea level). None of our land reaches such heights, so this means that there is no permanent snow in Britain. However, above this height, called the 'permanent snowline', the air temperature is too cold throughout the year and rain always falls as snow, and this snow never melts on any surface it lands on. Instead, as more snow falls, the snow lying underneath becomes compacted and turns to ice, eventually forming glaciers, like those we can visit in the Alps. Wales was a much colder place 170,000 years ago, and this permanent snowline in fact reached down to sea level. Extensive sheets of ice covered the country. This was only one of the several Ice Ages that have covered mid-Wales over the last 2 million years. Known as the Woolstonian, it lasted a mere 40,000 years, in geological terms a very short time. The country was covered in a thick, blue-white sheet of ice, reminiscent of Greenland today. Gilfach would have been a flat, stark, ice-bound, inhospitable place!

Glaciers are deceptive, appearing to be solid and immovable. Yet, then as now, these sheets of ice were not static. Rather they contained ice streams which, powered by gravity, moved slowly down the slope of the land beneath them. The might of the combination of the weight, texture and movement of a glacier cannot be rivalled by even the force of the largest river torrent. The Woolstonian ice streams bulldozed their way through the land carrying away with them fragments of rock and boulders. These, carried along under the ice streams, acted as gigantic nail files wearing away the craggy surfaces of the mountains and smoothing them into the undulating high plateau of which Gilfach is part.

The retreat of the Woolstonian ice was followed by a warmer period known as the Ipswichian interglacial period. As yet there has been no evidence found to suggest that man inhabited the country at this time. But we do know from fossilized bones that many animals did. Remains of species such as hippopotamus, fallow deer, wolf and lion have been found in mid-Wales. Their time here was to be limited for soon enough, a few thousand years later, an icy blast blew down the

WIND AND RAIN

Gilfach lies in the Cambrian mountains at a height of around 300 metres (984 feet) above sea level. As the crow flies, the site is only some 18.7 miles (20 kilometres) from the sea, in the path of the strong breezes coming from the Atlantic Ocean. Gilfach itself shelters in the rain-shadow of hills such as Plynlimon to the north-west. Because it is protected to some extent by the mountains, it actually receives less rain than does much of mid-Wales. In the upper reaches of the River Wye about 2,400 millimetres (94 inches) falls every year, but only around 1,700 millimetres (67 inches) falls in the Marteg area – this is the rain-shadow effect. About 85% of the rain and snow falling in the region comes from the frequent depression systems carried in on the Westerly Atlantic air streams. As these travel eastwards they meet the high ground of the Cambrian mountains and are forced upwards. This rise cools the air rapidly and it is no longer able to hold as much moisture, which is thus released as rain and snow onto the land, sheep and people below. Because the air stream reaches the higher slopes of Plynlimon first, it is here that most of the moisture is deposited.

While long wet spells do occur throughout the year, they are more likely in the spring and autumn. Rain falls on approximately 190-200 days a year, that is, around 53% of the year! Naturally, cloud cover is correspondingly high. Cloud cover is measured in oktas, an okta being $\frac{1}{8}$ of the sky. The average annual cloud cover around Gilfach is $\frac{6}{8}$, or $\frac{3}{4}$. Not surprisingly, the average amount of sunshine is low, only 1,300 hours per year, or roughly 3.5 hours a day.

Even in the finest spell, the day tends to start shrouded in a veil of morning mist, and the clouds tend to gather soon after sunset. In the nocturnal hours, clear skies are not falsely lit by manmade lights, but are deeply dark; dazzlingly pin-pricked with stars.

valley heralding another ice age. This was to last only 5,000 years, during which mammoth and woolly rhinoceros stalked the bleak and barren landscape. During this Upper Devensian period, the ice again covered the higher areas of Wales, forming ice caps. These ice caps spawned large glaciers which flowed along the existing river valleys, spilling over onto the adjacent higher ground. These valley glaciers were the agents responsible for the sculpted scenery we treasure as mid-Wales today.

At Gilfach, and all through the Wye-Marteg area, the signs of the ice are still visible to those who know what to look for. The direction of smoothing on rock projections and the presence of long, parallel scratches, called striations, chiselled in the rock tell us the flow direction of the glacial ice streams. These glaciers moved slowly and remorselessly down the Wye Valley, probably from a huge ice cap on the Plynlimon plateau to the north-west of Gilfach. The present River Wye flows along a valley which, in places, is deep and gorge-like. Such steep-sided valleys would have acted as retaining walls, constricting the passage of the ice and causing it to build up as more flowed down from the north. This, in turn, would have caused the ice to thicken and rise up the valley sides, producing the scraped

THE ICE AGE.

rock surfaces we can see over 180 metres (590 feet) above the valley floor.

Just as with water in river valleys, when the ice reached parts of the valley where the sides were not so steep or high it flowed over the shallower valley walls, thus escaping onto the adjacent ground. The Marteg valley was one such point and here the ice spilled over from the Wye Valley and forced its way up to the basin in the hills where now the village of St Harmon lies. This type of 'escaping' glacier is known as a 'diffluent glacier' and forms characteristically shaped valleys known as, not surprisingly, 'diffluent valleys' of which the Marteg valley is one.

The front of the Marteg glacier appears to have come to a halt in the St Harmon basin until some 13,000 years ago when the climate finally began to warm. The warmer weather meant that the ice started to melt at the surface and edges, particularly at the thinner St Harmon end. At the same time still more ice and rock rubbish fed into the Marteg ice stream from the Plynlimon ice cap. Thus, while the ice stream inside the glacier continued to flow forward, the overall size of the glacier was shrinking, with the shrinking being the faster process. This gave the impression of the ice beating a retreat. As the glacier gradually shrank back towards the junction with the Wye Valley, it began to drop its load, like an antisocial

---

tourist, depositing its rubbish as it went. This glacial rubbish of boulders and rocks is known as 'moraine' and between St Harmon and the Wye Valley we can see a series of low, crescent-shaped ridges known as 'terminal moraines', which indicate where the retreating glacier dumped its detritus when the weather got warmer. It is estimated that the glacier receded at a rate of 400 metres (1,312 feet) a year. It would have taken some 60 years to have retreated back to its Plynlimon source.

Another clue to the activities of the ice is the tops of the south-facing valley sides, which are all craggy. Whilst the ice smoothed the hills beneath it, it also served as a thick blanket protecting the underlying surface from the vagaries of the weather and, in particular, from snow and frost damage. However, the areas at the very tops of the hills that were not covered in ice were exposed to the sun, wind, frost and snow. These exposed summits are technically called 'nunataks'. Freezing conditions caused the tiny spaces throughout the rocks to expand as the droplets of water trapped in them froze into tiny ice crystals. Ice takes up more room than water and thus the crystals caused the rock to break up. Then warming from sunshine caused the ice particles to melt, leaving a slightly larger space than before. This space in turn would be filled with water seeping down into the rock. When the weather again cooled in the night, this water would freeze causing further expansion and break-up of the rock structure. The daily repetition of this freeze-thaw process finally caused fragments of the rocks to crack and to break off, forming crags. South-facing slopes would be more affected by freeze-thaw as the trapped ice crystals would melt more easily on these sunnier slopes, hence the craggy nature of the southern slopes of Wyloer Hill. No doubt the crag formation here was accentuated further by the plucking action of the ice flow. These slopes faced downstream of the ice flow and, as it moved past, the ice would have picked up bits of rock and carried them on its way, adding to the jagged, craggy outline.

As far as most of Britain is concerned, the last Great Ice Age ended some 13,000 years ago, though some ice stayed on for an extra 4,000 years in Snowdonia and northern Scotland. The term 'last ice age' may be a bit misleading as it is thought that we are living in another interglacial period, which is technically still part of the Ice Age. If this scenario is right then it is all too likely that Gilfach will once again be hidden beneath the ice. However, that is in the future and our story is concerned with the past.

As the climate warmed at the start of the Holocene, the ice slowly retreated and the land was exposed to a series of successive phases of vegetation colonization and of human activity leading to the modern Gilfach we now see. Of course plants need soil to grow, but when the ice retreated there was no soil, just ice-scoured, bare rock. Soil takes over 1,000 years to form and the type of soil that results depends on the underlying rock type, the local climate, local vegetation and slope of the land.

In the early stages of soil development, there is a high proportion of rock fragments compared to humus, which is largely composed of dead plant material. Such soils are known as 'skeletal'. They can be found where the surface is unstable because of the steepness of the slope; where the underlying rocks are too hard and where the temperature is too cold to allow any further development because of continued freeze-thaw. But even the rich, loamy soils of lowland Britain started out as skeletal soils.

The action of wind, rain and frost slowly and relentlessly breaks down the rock surfaces into tiny particles. The first living objects to colonize such bare rock surfaces are the lichens. Lichens can be seen all over Gilfach growing on rocks,

FLY AGARIC.

tree trunks and the stones of the buildings and walls. Different lichen species grow in a variety of shapes and colours. Being very susceptible to pollution, their profusion and the diversity of species in this part of the country is testimony to the relatively pollution-free atmosphere of the locality, helped by the prevailing winds bringing cleaner air from the Atlantic in the west rather than from the industrial Midlands to the east.

Whilst lichens look like single plants, in fact they are colonies of two quite different organisms growing together in an intimate association. These are a fungus and an alga, the fungus making up the bulk of the lichen with the alga buried within. Like animals, but unlike plants, fungi (including mushrooms and toadstools) are unable to make their own food and need a supply of organic food. Fungi tend to feed off the dead remains of other organisms or live as parasites on the living bodies of their hosts. The lichen fungi are unable to live independently and are highly specialized in their way of life, dependent on the living alga. In contrast to the lichen, the alga is a green plant and thus is a primary producer. This means that it is quite capable of manufacturing its own food from carbon dioxide (from the air), water (from rain and dew) and some simple minerals (from the underlying rock). In the lichen, then, the alga produces the food for both itself and the cohabiting fungus.

Lichens are extremely slow growing, increasing in size by only 2 to 20 millimetres (0.08 to 0.8 inches) a year. A long time would be needed for several of them just to cover a barn wall, let alone a mountainside. Many are circular in shape, growing from their edges outwards. One of the important and fascinating features of lichens is their ability to withstand being completely dried out for many months. In this dry state they can survive great extremes of heat and cold and, thus are often found on exposed bare rocks. Whilst dried out they are in a state of suspended animation, only continuing to grow when wetter conditions resume. Yet, though admirably able to cope with drought, lichens prefer a moist climate, which is another reason for the richness of the lichen population in the west of Britain.

Over hundreds of years the Gilfach lichens grew, reproduced and died, adding their organic matter to the primitive soils and so enriching them. As the soils became slightly more substantial and better able to hold moisture, they became suitable for colonization by mosses. This early moss and lichen landscape would have been similar to the vast expanses of tundra that still exist in many parts of the world, for example in Lappland, where they support herds of caribou, reindeer and many small mammals such as lemming. Since then, the soils have continued to build up and become richer in nutrients, though they are still considered poor in comparison to those in lowland Britain. Gradually, they were able to support a wider variety of life and over the millennia a succession of vegetation types have colonized Gilfach.

By 8,000 years ago the climate had improved somewhat and the tundra retreated northwards with pioneer species such as birch (*Betula*) colonizing behind and following its northerly progress. Close on the heels of the birch came Scots pine (*Pinus sylvestris*), hazel (*Corylus avellana*), some sessile oak (*Quercus petraea*) and scattered elm (*Ulmus*) and

SOILS AND BOGS

The climate, and in particular the high rainfall, affects both what is above ground and the soil below. None of the soils at Gilfach is particularly free draining because of the non–porous nature of the underlying rock. Naturally, on the steeper slopes gravity acts to help drain the area. The lack of sun and dry winds means that the rainwater evaporates slowly and that the area tends to be quite waterlogged. This in turn results in leaching. The water, working its way through the soil and down the hill, carries with it soluble nutrients from the soil. This causes the soils to become acidic and impoverished, with a pH of between 4 and 5. Not only does the water take nutrients, such as iron and lime, down the hillside, but also deeper into the soil itself, where they precipitate out, forming a relatively impermeable red or browny–orange layer called a 'pan'. Below this pan layer lies the rock, or parent material. These leached soils are known as 'podzols', after the Russian word '*zola*' meaning ashes. This conjures up an image of a layer of grey which indeed is the characteristic colour of the leached layer of these soils, found just beneath the surface layer of black humus.

Because of the wetness and acidity dead plants do not break down easily, and podzols on the slopes tend to have only a thin top layer of humus. On the flatter land the soil may become quite waterlogged and stagnant, therefore low in oxygen. The acidity of the water, resembling vinegar, and the low amount of oxygen results in an extremely slow rate of decay of the dead plants. These partially decayed plants form what is known as peat. As successive generations grow and die on the remains of their forebears, these layers of peat can mature to depths of several metres. At the bottom of the

small hill at Gilfach the peat is 1.5 metres (5 feet) deep. Extensive areas can form what are known as 'mat' or 'blanket bogs', covering whole hilltops. If cut into blocks and allowed to dry, the peat can be used as fuel, and many fires used to burn this natural fuel throughout the British uplands. The high organic content of the peat also makes it attractive to gardeners and it is a conservation issue of our time that we are destroying vast areas of upland and lowland peatland, far more than when local people used it for burning.

Some water, trickling through the soil, re-emerges at the surface part way down the slope. The point where the water re-surfaces is called a 'flush' and can take the form of a spring, or rivulet, or merely a damp area where the water comes nearer to the surface, bringing its cargo of nutrients and fine soil particles with it. Such areas are thus richer and can be visually located by patches of greener vegetation on the hillside.

At the foot of the hill, in the valleys, the soil tends to be deeper as it accumulates through soil creep. Often the ground is again quite flat and becomes waterlogged, resulting in thick layers of valley peat, perhaps 2 metres (6.5 feet) or more in depth.

Only a few specialized plant species can cope with the high acidity and low nutrient levels of these upland soils. This is reflected in what are called the 'capability values' designated to them by the Ministry of Agriculture. The flatter tops and peaty slopes are rated at 5, which is very poor and of little agricultural use. Those soils of the steeper side slopes and peaty valley accumulations rate, at best, 3; denoting good grassland potential but little potential for growing crops.

alder (*Alnus glutinosa*). Much of what we know of the succession of plants in Britain comes from the pollen record, that is the microscopic identification of pollen grains trapped in different layers of soil. From this record we know that over Britain the birch woods grew in size, gradually to be supplanted by Scot's pine, which for several hundred years became the dominant species.

Some 7,000 years ago the climate changed again, becoming substantially warmer and wetter than it is now. This period is known as the 'climatic optimum' and lasted about 2,500 years. It is known as the optimum because of the favourable conditions it provided for plant growth, as reflected in the development of the wildwood still fabled in our mythology. By definition wildwood is woodland, or forest, that has never been interfered with by man. None now remains in Britain, though some ancient woods are descended from the wildwood.

During the period of climatic optimum the broadleaved trees for which Britain is so famous began to take hold. Species such as sessile oak and pedunculate oak (*Quercus robur*), alder and hazel became common. The two oak species succeeded as the most important species, and continue to do so, with the sessile oak holding sway in the uplands and its cousin ruling the lowland regions. New colonists also began to appear such as rowan, or mountain ash (*Sorbus*), hawthorn (*Crataegus*), willow (*Salix*), aspen (*Populus*) and the 'bearer of the woodland crown' the holly (*Ilex*).

The period between about 8,500 and 6,300 years ago was the era of Mesolithic man. Archaeologists have found evidence that these Middle Stone Age people had camps up at the treeline in the uplands, rather then where one might imagine on the more sheltered lower slopes. But, remember, the forest would have been home to many predators such as bear and wolf, dangerous to men as well as animal prey. Living on the upper slopes, based at the upper treeline, also made strategic sense. It provided a better position, nearer the herds of deer grazing the open land above the trees. The pollen record tells us that these early people also undertook small-scale clearing of the trees at the treeline. This would have enabled them to create grassy glades which would have been attractive to grazing and browsing deer, providing sites where the deer could be ambushed. It is unlikely that Mesolithic man created these glades using the slash-and-burn techniques we associate with modern forest clearance. Oak and other broadleaved species do not burn easily, especially in the rather wet climate of Britain at the time! It is more likely that the trees were ringbarked, that is a deep cut was made in the bark right around the tree, stopping the flow of nutrients up the tree and causing it to die.

Once dead, the tree could more easily be felled with stone axes and burned. We can also speculate on other activities of these people from what the pollen record tells us. We know that there was an abundance of hazel pollen in these areas and it may well be that man had begun to coppice the hazel. Coppicing is the regular cutting of the tree back to ground level. This encourages new growth which would have provided accessible new shoots and leaves for browsing deer.

RAMSON

While the clearings created by Mesolithic people were only small, over a period of 2,000 years they would have had quite an effect on the future extent of the wildwood. The burning of the dead ringbarked trees would initially have improved the soil by adding to it the nutrients contained in the tree ash. However, the removal of cover and tree and plant roots, which bind the soil, would leave the area more vulnerable to the eroding elements. Those clearings up near the treeline were even more exposed to the stronger winds and higher rainfall, which marked the end of the climatic optimum about 4,500 years ago. The action of wind and rain would have resulted in substantial erosion of the young soils, slowly washing them downhill. Likewise, rainwater trickling through the unprotected soil would have rinsed out, or leached, the precious nutrients, again carrying them downhill, and farther afield down the streams and rivers. During the climatic optimum there was a particularly wet phase, during which leaching was exacerbated by the heavy rainfall, and the sodden conditions meant there was little opportunity for insects and fungi to break down dead plants. This led to the formation of deep and extensive layers of peat, the ubiquitous blanket bogs of the British uplands, in which preserved trunks of trees can be found. This blanket bog had a serious impact on the wildwood, the heritage of which is still with us. It meant that the resulting habitat was no longer suitable for trees and the treeline was gradually pushed further down.

Had the destruction not continued, then the trees might have regained their upland foothold; but the destruction not only continued, it became more intense. The arrival of the Neolithic peoples heralded the dawning of a new turn in the progress of mankind. The Neolithic period stretched from about 6,300 to 4,200 years ago and is characterized by being, among other things, the first major period of forest recession. No longer was clearing conducted on a small, local scale by groups of people following the annual movements of the wild herds. Now, in this the period of the climatic optimum and establishment of the broadleaf species, man began to change his lifestyle: from being a hunter-gatherer, he began to settle in relatively large communities, and start to farm the land. Not only did he grow crops but he also tended herds of domestic pigs and small, black cattle, both descended from the wild stock already present. It is unlikely that these people had any great number of domestic sheep. Sheep are animals of open grasslands and short sward, and as yet the country was still heavily wooded. Also, sheep are among the most defenceless of creatures and would have been easy prey for marauding packs of wolves. The early domestic sheep that were contemporary with Neolithic man are called Turbary or peat sheep (*Ovis aries palustris*), and we know from archaeological remains that they were small, slender-legged and sported curved, goatlike horns which would give better protection than the twisted horns of modern sheep.

Whilst living a distinctly more settled life, the Neolithics were still semi-nomadic, partly because their farming practices soon exhausted the soils and partly because they were still dependent to some extent on hunting. Those living in the upland areas also practised the transhumance tradition common to mountain people all over the world, even today. In Wales, this is known as '*Hafod-Hendre*' and comprises the moving of cattle or sheep to upland pastures to graze in the summer months, whilst the shepherds live nearby in the '*Hafodty*' or summer house. In the autumn the animals are moved to lower, sheltered fields near the '*Hendre*', the more solidly constructed winter house. The population of Britain grew during the Neolithic period and with it grew the size of the herds. The increased need for temporary clearings for villages, pasture land and fields meant the wildwood was destroyed at a greater rate than ever before. Due to the semi-nomadic lifestyle, clearings were often abandoned and some no doubt were reclaimed by the forest. Others, however, were under sufficient grazing pressure from wild and domestic herbivores that grassland plants were able to colonize them; thus the British landscape opened up. Over a few hundred years Neolithic man, apparently often using slash-and-burn as well as ringbarking, caused a major decline in elm, oak, ash and lime (*Tilia*) both in upland and lowland Britain. This further ensured the encroachment of bog and reduction of soil quality in the upland areas, whilst in lowland areas such as Surrey and Hampshire the heathland made great advances.

Throughout the country our Neolithic forebears have left traces of their homes, trackways and burial grounds. One such ancient trackway, known as the Monk's

Trod, runs through Gilfach on its eastward journey towards Abbeycwmhir. There is also a prehistoric tumulus or cairn on the southern slope of Wyloer Hill just above the road. It is not known whether the site is a burial place or a landmark. Whichever, such remains are fairly obvious signs of habitation by early man. A more subtle relic is the open moorland we see about us.

The Neolithic or Stone Age culture came to an end about 4,200 years ago with the arrival of the Bronze Age which lasted 1,700 years. These people came from the Netherlands and Rhineland areas of Europe and bought with them a new breed of sheep which had massive spiral horns, and was probably a domesticated form of the mouflon — a breed now only found in Corsica and Sardinia. They continued to produce small clearances for grazing and crop growing purposes. More importantly they brought a revolutionary new technology: that of making tools and weapons from the metal alloy, bronze. During the Bronze Age the demand for wood as a fuel was greater than at any previous time in Britain's history. Not only was the population larger, but also the smelting of copper and tin to produce the bronze exacted a heavy load on the local woodland. During the Bronze Age the climate became warmer and drier and increasingly man, with his new tools, was able to cultivate the upland areas. He divided the land up with long stone walls, clearing the fields of stones and dumping them in piles, which we know as cairns and can still see dotting the landscape of the uplands.

In addition to small-scale clearances, Bronze Age man undertook large scale clearing by extensive burning of the wildwood. Certainly such burning fulfilled the task of removing the trees, but it also killed off many of the seeds in the soil. This population of unsprouted seeds is known as the seed bank and is essential for the regeneration of an area of cleared land. The grazing of the land by sheep and cattle also suppresses regeneration as the animals continually munch any tree seedlings that start to grow. At the same time, the exposed soil is being washed or blown away, slowly creeping downhill and losing its nutrients as they are leached out. One result of all this is the type of woodland we in Britain have inherited. A wood here that contains fifteen or more plant and tree species is considered rich in vegetation, whereas there are literally hundreds of different plants found in tropical forests. The Channel was and is a barrier to the migration of plants and animals from the Continent, but man's activities may also have caused the species-poor woodlands of Britain. A sobering thought, given the level of pillage that we, modern man, are committing on woodland all around the world, making the activities of our forebears look inconsequential.

Unlike modern forest clearance activities, the Bronze Age clearance would have taken many generations. The removal of the woodland would have had the effect of driving many species of animal, as well as plant, to local extinction. Certainly, the number of predator species would have decreased, allowing for an increase in the number and importance of sheep.

About 2,500 years ago the Iron Age people arrived. These Celtic tribes came from Belgium and, like those before them, they displaced the resident peoples. The Celts lived a much more settled existence than their predecessors. They lived in stable territories, villages if you like, and made their livings from farming. With their stronger tools they were able to clear the heavy soils of the lowlands and they settled all over Britain. Julius Caesar, when he invaded south-east England just over 2,000 years ago, in 55 BC, described their villages as numbering several hundred people, including the Celtic craftsmen renowned for their jewellery. Individual Celtic communities formed strong allegiances with a wider group and tribes, such as the Silures and Ordovices, were the usual extended community system rather than the small hunter-gatherer family groups of the Bronze Age. It was these well organized, but ultimately undisciplined agricultural peoples with their iron tools and weapons that greeted Claudius as he began his assault on Wales.

The upland terrain of Wales, with its hidden valleys and remote hilltops, acted as a protective barrier for its people. Whilst the Romans and, later, the Normans, managed to occupy much of the country, there was little in the way of social integration and the Welsh (as they were later to be called), then as now, clung strongly to their cultural heritage. The Romans brought with them better farming technology, in particular a superior ploughshare. This enabled the indigenous people to settle and farm the deeper soils of the valleys, resulting in extensive destruction of the valley woodlands.

By AD400, 1,600 years ago, the Romans had left Britain and the country as a whole entered a period that used to be known as the Dark Ages. This era lasted some 600 years to around AD1000 and was so called because there was little in the way of written records of the time. However, thanks to developments in archaeological techniques, we now know far more about this period and the term Dark Ages is no longer applicable. In Wales the population, no longer oppressed or having the 'northmen' as a common enemy, indulged in inter-tribal warfare with the eventual division of the country into four kingdoms, of which Powys was one.

In the early part of the 10th century Hywel Dda, king of Deheubarth in the south, conquered Powys. Hywel Dda's name translates as 'The Good' and he was indeed a forward thinking, peaceful man and great admirer of his contemporary, Alfred the Great of Wessex (and of burnt cake fame!). He attempted to make Wales a fair and law-abiding country by formulating and codifying a set of laws, written in both Welsh and Latin, which, 900 years ago, put Wales in the forefront of social reform. For instance, his laws were the first in Europe to recognize that women were not merely chattels but were entitled to human rights, and that commoner and king were of equal worth, saying that 'The hand of the bondsman is the same worth as the king's hand.' Indeed, various parts of the body were given a value to be paid if mutilated. The loss of a finger, or of its use, was worth a cow, whilst the mutilation of a foot or nose incurred the fine of 120 pieces of silver plus six cattle. The laws tried to cover all possible eventualities of rural community living and were based on a straightforward logic. For example, taking the scenario that a pig wandered into a home, knocked over the fire and set the building ablaze, two outcomes were possible. If the pig survived then the pig's owner had to pay compensation, but, if the pig perished in the fire, then no fine was due. For, as the law says 'if the swine be burnt, then both swine and house are equal, for both are stupid' – and who could argue with that!

One of the more important laws of Hywel Dda was the system of inheritance he introduced. Recorded as 'gavelkind', this was theoretically an uncommonly fair system, whereby the male heirs inherited their father's land in equal portions, equality not only judged by size but also by quality of land. This was splendid in theory but in fact resulted in infighting between heirs as lands became progressively more fragmented over the 500 years before the law was repealed by the Act of Union in 1536. A combination of the difficulties in farming the terrain, the gavelkind system and the Enclosures Acts are responsible for the generally small size of Welsh farms, such as Gilfach.

DANDELION

Because the Welsh kinglets spent much of their time squabbling with each other rather than looking to external enemies, the Welsh borderlands were easy targets for the invading Normans. There was of course resistance and in the Gilfach area two men, Rhys ap Gruffedd and Cadwallon, bravely led the movement against the Normans. In 1170, Rhys built a castle at Rhayader which was occupied by the Normans after his death in 1197. But the resistance movement continued and in 1231 the castle and its Norman inhabitants were destroyed by Llywelyn ap Iorweth, only 60 years after it had been built. Rhys ap Gruffedd and Cadwallon left another mark on the area, namely the Cistercian abbeys of Strata Florida and Abbeycwmhir, to whom they gave large tracts of land. The Elan Valley, directly to the west of Gilfach, was part of the grant Rhys made to the monks of Strata Florida. Throughout Wales there were many small monastic settlements, but those of Strata Florida and Abbeycwmhir were large and, in their time, powerful.

The monks were basically farmers of sheep, cattle and pigs. Whilst the monks lived in the abbeys, the lay members farmed the land, living in small communities with their families. The two abbeys were closely connected both spiritually and physically, and the Monk's Trod acted as a linkway across the intervening mountains. As mentioned earlier, this ancient road probably dates back to prehistoric times and wends part of its way through Gilfach, passing along the hillside behind the house. During the 12th century, sheep farming became and continued to be the principal industry of the country and wool its most important export. Certainly the monks of Strata Florida and Abbeycwmhir exported wool to France and Flanders.

The era of peace and prosperity enjoyed by these religious houses came to an abrupt end in 1401 when Henry IV, then Duke of Lancaster, brought off a successful coup against Richard II for the English throne. Unfortunately, the Mortimers, a Norman family, complicated the proceedings by claiming the throne for themselves and waging war with Henry, dragging into the fray the Welsh leader Owain Glyndwr who was fighting for an independent Wales. Both the abbeys, in particular Abbeycwmhir, suffered and were seriously reduced in power during the following troubled century. Peace was regained at last in the mid-1500s under the rule of Henry VIII. An important tool in the restoration of peace was the Act of Union which brought Wales firmly under English rule, revoking the laws of Hywel Dda. Sadly, Henry VIII also finally put to ruin Strata Florida and Abbeycwmhir during the Reformation .

The Monk's Trod, however, continued in its importance as a linkway and a drover's route. As transport and communication systems were poor, communities were basically self-sufficient and the hills would have been more populated than they are now with farmers, craftsmen and tradesmen. The drovers were pivotal to the community. These honest men were essential for the continuation of the economy of these scattered villages. They were the forerunners of freight trains and road transport. With their ponies and dogs they herded, or drove, sheep and cattle and carried exports, such as wool, to the markets of England. Back to the homeland they brought money from their sales, cloth, salt, goods and news. The cavalcades of several hundred beasts would traverse the distance at a speed of around 3 kilometres an hour (1.8 miles) covering maybe only 30 kilometres (18.6 miles) in a day. A one-way trip from Gilfach to the markets of London would have taken about 2 weeks. Much of the route used the ancient trackways, such as the Monk's Trod, and many overnight stops were required. Catering for these men and beasts could prove a useful form of income for farmers located along the way. Those offering accommodation and grazing advertised the fact by planting a group of three Scots pines somewhere prominent; in England yew trees were often used instead.

In the 1700s there was an attempt to improve the roads which necessitated the establishment of tollgates. The tolls exacted for using the roads were expensive and the discontent caused eventually resulted in riots throughout the country and not least in Rhayader. These were known as the Rebecca Riots of 1843-4.

In the 1860s, the natural sounds of the hills were rudely shattered by the arrival of the railway and the opening up of the area to the outside world and tourists. Although the railway was of importance to the economy of Wales, it did not really impinge on everyday life. Similarly, up until the late 1940s many roads, especially those leading to more remote farms, were unsuitable for cars. Doctors would visit their patients by horseback, stitching cuts and setting bones in the patient's own home, probably on the kitchen table — well scrubbed for the purpose.

Now in the sunset of the 20th century, the apparent restrictions of railway travel and poor roads have been superseded by our need for independence of movement (and love of sitting in traffic jams?). Stretches of well maintained main roads have overtaken the travel importance of the trackways and winding lanes. The harsh cutback of the railway system in the 1960s has led to a greater reliance on the car both in Wales and all over Britain. Many wish for a renewal of public transport systems, especially in these remote areas where not everyone can afford, or desires to be dependant on the car.

2

HOMES FOR MEN AND ANIMALS

Over the centuries Gilfach has been modified by man to serve his purposes, within the limits dictated by the underlying geology and climate. Even with modern technology, inhabitants of hill farms are still constrained by the vagaries of their natural environs more than we might think. These forces affect the type of farming and the social and cultural heritage of the region is a response to local climate, materials and way of life.

Architectural conservation used to be concerned mainly with houses of the wealthy and famous; buildings of the common man, whether rural or urban, were often demolished or modernized beyond recognition and much has been lost. Gilfach farmhouse represents one of a now rare type of rural dwelling. It is to the credit of our changing attitudes that this building is to be preserved and employed in the conservation of Gilfach as a whole.

The house at first glance may not look special; it was, when I first saw it, in a pathetic state of decay and neglect. However, it is a representative of a basic building type, the utilitarian and economic longhouse. This was once common, not only in western Radnorshire, but across Great Britain and much of Europe. The importance of Gilfach farmhouse is that, though adapted and extended in the 17th and 19th centuries, the original longhouse plan remains. The house was unoccupied from the mid 1960s until 1990. The final decade of the century will see a 'light' restoration by the Radnorshire Wildlife Trust to a form similar to that when it was last inhabited.

A track from the road crosses the old railway bridge over the Marteg River and climbs up the hill to approach the house from the south, such that you pass its west end into the yard. The main body of the house looks across the slope of the hill. Aesthetically, one would expect it to face down the slope and look out across the valley, but to the builders of such houses the direction of the prevailing wind and the sun was of prime importance . The house is built on a medieval platform site, cut into the hillside at a relatively flat point. The main length of the house being on the east/west axis means there is less area to bear the brunt of the prevailing westerly winds. This orientation also means that as little area as possible is exposed to water coming downhill (damp proof coursing was not as good as it purports to be nowadays!). To the north, facing the house, is an 18th century barn which, together with the house and hillside, form the three sides of the yard. Along-

GILFACH FARM BUILDINGS UNDER RESTORATION.

———

side is a supply of fresh spring water which is stored in a cistern located under a paved wellhead at the south-east corner of the yard.

Before entering the house it is worth spending a few moments getting acquainted with its external appearance. Standing in the yard, facing the north side, it is easy to see why this design is known as a longhouse. The rectangular shape was intended to shelter both humans and livestock, the latter especially during the winter months. The building was roughly divided up into $\frac{1}{3}$ for humans and $\frac{2}{3}$ for animals, the 17th-century chimney now approximately marking this divide. The human end is upslope, to the east, presumably so that any leakage from the livestock area flowed away down the hill. Having the livestock in the same building provided a means of heating the house as their body heat would permeate through to the human part, as no doubt did their aromas!

The roof was originally constructed from locally obtained slates known as 'strongs' or 'seconds'. These were thick slates of a quality intermediate between the thin 'first' quality Welsh slates of more prosperous homes and the stone tiles typical of south-east Wales. The restoration of Gilfach has used 'seconds' as far as possible, many from the original roof. In the 17th century various additions were made to the building, including the chimney – previously there would have just been a hole in the roof. The chimney is notable for its 'roof leeks', no relation to the Welsh national emblem. These stone projections halfway down the stack were intended to protect the chimney/roof joint from water damage. If you go into the house, take a look at the fireplace, which is offset from the chimney, an arrangement characteristic of this period and region. Also during the 17th century two dormer windows were inserted in the roof. The one to the east lit the upper room of the domestic end when the parlour wing, with its upper floor and internal partitioning, was added. The right hand, western, window was originally not a window at all, but a dormered doorway to the hayloft, accessible from a cart. Just above the window are a series of holes leading into the pigeon loft, the birds providing a source of fresh meat in the winter.

Also visible from this side are four doorways, the three to the west leading to the cowhouse and the most easterly to the house. The latter has been the main entrance to the house since the 1600s. Because of the installation of the chimney at this time, this door was placed slightly upslope of the original, whose jamb can be seen on the inside of the wall. It is likely that only one of the three entrances to the byre is original, but I'm not guessing which! In the 19th century the middle one led onto a 'feedwalk', a raised path through the building enabling the farmer to feed the animals without getting his feet dirty. The outer two led to tethering areas for the cattle.

Moving upslope to the east end of the house a surprise is in store, two beautiful timber-framed gables tucked up against the hillside, a rare survival in the Radnorshire uplands. These were part of the 17th-century improvements, when the longhouse's original cruck construction was adapted and the timber-framed walls were replaced by stone. The window to the right, north side is situated in the original gable end of the longhouse as evidenced by the unusual asymmetric framing of the gable. The left-hand gable projects from the parlour wing extension. It is dramatically embellished in black and white with close studded vertical framing below the window and decorative diamond framing above. All these additions and external decoration imply that Gilfach was quite a prosperous farm in the 17th century.

Turning to the south side, you face the end of the parlour wing. Normally, this extension would have been added to the main line of the building, at the east end. At Gilfach the lie of the land made this impossible and the parlour was placed at right angles to the original longhouse. Mind you, but for this compromise, there would have been no room for the two fancy timber-framed gables. The parlour retains its original fireplace and its decorative moulding.

To the left of the parlour chimney, in the longhouse proper, is a window. This marks the site of the original door leading into the raised cross passage connecting to the door on the north side mentioned earlier. Before the

---

TREND SETTING HOMES

The longhouse became the common rural dwelling during the Middle Ages and continued to be built up to the 19th century. Though there were regional differences, many longhouses followed a pattern known as 'cruck construction' or 'cruck houses'. These were revolutionary in that they were the forerunners of prefabricated, commercially produced, timber-framed buildings, bringing sizeable homes within reach of most people. Prior to cruck houses, poorer families built their own homes from wood, stone or clay. Such homes would have been small as construction was extremely labour intensive. Cruck houses on the other hand, could be brought in, reducing individual labour costs and were large and sturdy . . . as the long life of Gilfach testifies.

The frame was made from wooden structures known as crucks. These were built from split sections of suitably large and well shaped trees, notably oak, the trunks forming the wall supports and the bough curves the roof supports. The splitting of each tree section resulted in two matching pieces, a cruck couple, which could be joined together forming the outline of the building. In between the wall struts were placed timber beams infilled with wattle and daub. The carpentry involved required a great deal of skill and would have been performed in the nearest timber yard. All the segments would have been clearly marked as to the order in which they would be put together on site, a feat performed by skilled labourers known as 'spider men'. The same basic pattern , turned upside-down, was used in the building of ships.

17th-century additions, this passage marked the divide between humans and animals and is a characteristic feature of the longhouse design. Further along the south wall a lean-to was added in the 19th century, now, with the Trust's restoration plans, to be retained as the public toilets.

A second, preserved, lean-to, dating from the 19th century can be seen on the west end facing the trackway. This appears to have been used as a storage area and a slaughterhouse. It is raised several feet off the ground, keeping it away from the damp, and divided into two parts, a larger open area and a small animal stall. The latter was probably used to house the family pig for fattening. On the outer side of the stall was a tin sheet with a shallow stone bowl below. The sheet acted as a splash board and blood was collected in the bowl to be used later in the making of sausages.

The restoration of the longhouse will again split it into two parts, the east end remaining for human accommodation and the byre being used as an interpretation area. Here part of an original 'cruck couple' can be seen in the south wall, and in the Reception area there is a fine post and panel partition and coffered ceiling with chamfered beams and ogee stops.

It is difficult to fully appreciate the relationship between Gilfach's buildings and the local environment without having some feeling for the life led by the inhabitants. So I would like to paint you a brief picture of farming life in these hills. This lifestyle has changed little over the generations, continuing well into the 20th century.

Originally, Gilfach would have been virtually self-sufficient with both arable and livestock farming. Now, fewer cattle are seen on the upland pastures and more feedstuffs, for human and animal consumption, are bought in rather than being home produced. Otherwise, much about the character of hill farming follows an age-old pattern.

For many of us, farming conjures up scenes of tranquillity, far removed from the stresses of the rat race. Certainly, the pace of life in these hills is more gentle than in the town or city. Sitting on Wyloer Hill on a warm summer's day, watching the larks (*Alauda arvensis*) above and the sheep below, one can be lulled into believing that it was and will always be this idyl-

ABOVE STONE 'BLOOD' BOWL FOUND AT GILFACH.

ONE OF THE TIMBER-FRAMED GABLES AT GILFACH, PRIOR TO RESTORATION.

lic. But the winters are harsh and can be severe, blizzards can rage and roads become impassable for days at a time.

The farming year starts in October with the stock sales. At markets such as in nearby Rhayader, the year's lambs and excess adults are sold. Hill farming economy relies on the breeding rather than the rearing of sheep, as animals reared for meat fatten up much quicker on the richer grasses of lowland pastures. Up on the hills the sheep need to be of a hardy breed, such as the Welsh Mountain or Beulah Speckled Face, able to live in the harsh conditions and on the low quality grazing.

Rams are put to the ewes in November, ensuring the lambs are born in April when there is plenty of spring growth to keep both mother and young healthy and ensure that the ewe can provide a plentiful supply of milk. Autumn is also the time when preparations are made for the winter. Though only a few miles from Rhayader, Gilfach is often snowbound. With today's supply of tinned and frozen foods, preparing for such an eventuality is not so difficult. But as recently as the 1930s such preparations entailed many hours of hard labour. Most farms, Gilfach included, ran cattle as well as sheep and often would have had a few pigs. These pigs would have been fattened up during the spring and summer and slaughtered in the autumn, the meat preserved by being salted. Bars of rock salt were rubbed into the meat, making sure the salt permeated right through and, incidentally, into the salter's hands, making them quite raw.

In our 'high tech' age we do not think much of providing light on a dark evening, we merely flick the switch. However, while still in use as a farm, Gilfach was never connected to the local electricity supply. In the 1960s all the farmers in the Marteg valley shared the cost of having electricity connected, but, for reasons best known to himself, Mr Hughes, the last owner, only had the electricity brought to the farmhouse door. It was not installed in the house until he had moved else-where. Perhaps he preferred the softer, traditional light of rushlights, candles and paraffin lamps (though there is some evidence, from a pipe found in the reception area, that gas, probably bottled, was available). Paraffin lamps were comparatively expensive but provided a stronger light than the cheaper rushlights and candles which tended to be homemade. Rushes (*Juncaceae*) were gathered from boggy areas and stripped of all but part of the stiff outer stem, the remaining segment acting as a support for the rushlight. They were then drawn slowly through melted pig fat which soaked into the soft pith. Candles burned more slowly than rushlights, and took longer to make. Lengths of wick were cut and hung on a wire. These were then dipped in melted sheep's fat (tallow), straightened and left to harden before being dipped again. This was repeated thirty times or more before a suitably thick candle was made.

As sure as night follows day, winter follows autumn. This is the time when the cattle were brought into the byre to spend the long, cold months tethered in the warm, semi-darkness. With the store of winter feed above in the hayloft and both animals and feedstuffs being just a corridor away, the longhouse system meant that tending the cattle during the winter was made as easy as possible. The sheep, however, were, and still are, left to fend for themselves to a far greater extent. Hardy and wrapped in thick fleeces, they are better able to cope with the weather, but even they need help. If the snow is too deep for them to forage then they are provided with hay. Deeper, drifting snow might necessitate long hard hours rescuing stranded sheep.

The traditional winter feed for both cattle and sheep is hay, made from grasses cut after they have flowered and dried in the warm sun. The weather is of vital importance to hay making for, if baled up when too wet, the grass may start to ferment and overheat as it slowly dries. This could cause it to combust spontaneously – risking the whole crop and the building in which it is stored. Hay is usually taken from fields left ungrazed during the summer growing season; these meadows are known as hay meadows and some of the little fields at Gilfach are managed this way. An alternative is to use the purple moor grass (*Molinia caerulea*) from the upland slopes which makes a rougher, less nutritious feed called rhos hay.

More recently, the trend in agriculture has shifted to the feeding of silage. This is made from grasses cut earlier in the season and packed either into dark silage pits or huge black plastic bags. Here the grass ferments over the summer into a smelly, soggy and mildly alcoholic concoction; perhaps it is this last quality that makes it so attractive to sheep and cattle! Unfortunately, silage is not so good for wildlife. Silage is cut before grass and associated herbs have had time to flower and set seed. This means that for many meadow plant species, such as ragged robin (*Lychnis flos-cuculi*), yellow rattle (*Rhianthus minor*) and burnet saxifrage (*Pimpinella saxifraga*), silage-making spells local extinction. The lack of flowers also means a lack of food and breeding sites for many insects and ground-nesting birds.

Nowadays, cattle are less common in the uplands but in years gone by the milder days of spring signalled their release into the pastures to feed on the sweet early grass. Then and now, the spring air resounds to the plaintive bleating of

GILFACH UNDER RESTORATION, 1991, PROTECTED BY CORRUGATED SHEETING.

lambs and the husky replies of their mothers, keeping track of each other as they wander over the sward. Lambs are born at all hours during April and May, later than in the warmer lowlands. It is a busy time for farmers, helping ewes who have trouble giving birth and caring for orphaned youngsters. The lambs themselves are at risk from birds of prey and crows (*Corvus*). While buzzard (*Buteo buteo*) and red kite (*Milvus milvus*) tend to eat carrion, the crows are more ruthless, plucking the eyes from both lambs and ewes who are defenceless when giving birth.

Unlike on lowland farms, hill sheep are not kept in fenced pastures but are allowed to roam free. Sheep are born on the hill and tend to stay near where they grew up. Some do stray, especially those at the margins of two neighbouring flocks, but these are sorted at the summer gatherings. At the first gathering, or round-up,

LONG-TAILED TITS EXPLORING THE UNRESTORED GILFACH LONGHOUSE.

the lambs are sexed and ear-marked, and most male lambs are castrated. These 'wethers' grow faster and will be ready for the table in the autumn while the remaining male lambs ('tups') are left to become flock studs.

In July the sheep are sheared, traditionally a co-operative venture with neighbouring farmers helping each other. In the past a seasoned shearer using hand-shears, resembling gigantic scissors, could separate a sheep from its wool in five minutes. Nowadays, using modern electric shears, this is accomplished in just one. Progress continues to march on and it is possible that shearing as such will

FOR BETTER AND FOR WORSE

In rural Wales distances between farms and cottages, especially if you did not have a pony, were daunting. For a suitor this posed a problem. Work was hard and for many farmers there was little time free to go a-wooing, perhaps one evening a week. The lady of your dreams might live a five or even ten mile walk away. In addition, most homes were small and the family lived and slept in a single room, thereby reducing the use of firewood, or peat, and precious rushlights. As described by one historian, a bed of rushes was placed on the floor and covered with a coarse cloth called a 'brychan'. All the members of the household lay down on this bed, without changing their clothes. The fire was kept burning throughout the night and the sleepers kept warm by huddling together. I suspect that this was not a particularly comfortable arrangement and it certainly wasn't conducive to long evenings talking and getting to know your intended.

The functional necessity of this group sleeping arrangement was overlooked by later observers, who considered it the reason for 'the great moral laxness among the population, with an absence of feminine delicacy among the women'. As in similarly sparsely distributed, and poor populations throughout Europe, Scandinavia and the North Americas, there developed the courtship practice of 'bundling'. Once again, an aspect of man's life in part determined by the harshness of the climate.

Bundling was a normal, but not inevitable, preliminary to marriage. There were regional variations on the custom; basically the courting couple spent a night (or several) together in the same bed, fully clothed, where they could continue their courtship without burning candles needlessly. The girl would have been sewn into her clothing as an added precaution. The practice was usually restricted to those couples who were engaged, or at least had intentions of marrying. There was little in the way of abuse of the system, no doubt in part because of the presence of the rest of the family in the room and, also, because of the consequences of such an indiscretion. Bundling was an ancient custom, commented on by Caesar, who considered the Britons polygamists. However, by the 19th century the custom was rapidly dying out as being 'not decent and unChristian'. It became more sophisticated to have settees in the home and to let the young couple sit and chat the night away, though many maintained there was more sinning on settees than in the bundle-bed. Perhaps a reflection of the innocence of the system was the custom on marriage of the husband giving his wife a present, called the 'cowyll', on the morning after the consummation of the marriage; a present in return for her maidenhood.

A Welsh woman living in the 11th and 12th centuries was luckier than most of her contemporaries should her marriage not work out. At this time in history, marriage for most European and British women was little better than slavery. However, thanks to the enlightenment of Hywel Dda, Welsh women were recognized as having rights of their own. Hywel Dda accepted that not all marriages would last, and wrote the seven-year-itch into law. If a woman left her husband in the first seven years, she had no claim to any of his property – unless she could show good cause for leaving him. Amongst other acceptable reasons were impotence and bad breath! Should the marriage break up after the seventh year, then the woman was entitled to the blankets off the marriage bed, the sheep and any pickled meat, whilst the husband retained the mattress, pigs, any hung meat and of course the house. It all seems a lot more civilized than some of the divorce court battles we hear of nowadays.

become obsolete. Agricultural researchers in Australia are developing a protein injection which will inhibit wool growth for a day or so. Then a few weeks later, when the wool has grown a bit, the fleece can literally be pulled off the sheep's back. I guess it will be quieter than all those electric shears buzzing, but I don't see this new technology at Gilfach for a while yet.

This ancient annual rhythm to which the inhabitants of Gilfach had lived their lives for centuries was, for a mere hundred years, rudely shattered by the faster pace of the industrial age.

Passing through Gilfach, like the track of a meandering snail, runs part of the remains of the Mid-Wales line. The railway engineers, as did the road-makers before them, chose the flattest route available. This meant following the course of the river as far as possible, the river having done much of the work for them by cutting through the rock in the preceding millennia. From the road it is easy to follow the railway track as it makes its way from Marteg Bridge, past Gilfach and on up the valley to St Harmon. For a short distance it disappears under the mountain, cutting off the loop of the river by Ffwrd Falls. Here the hardness of the rock and steepness of the bank left no option to the engineers other than to cut a tunnel through the rock … by hand!

Disused since the 1960s, the line has been incorporated into the fabric of the Gilfach reserve. The deep layer of ballast is better drained than the surrounding earth, thus providing a specialized habitat suitable for plants that like dry, well drained and nutrient-poor conditions, such as ragwort (*Senecio jacobaea*) and the rarer small toadflax (*Chaenorhinum minus*). In the late summer and autumn, a profusion of fungi grow on the banks either side of the track. As in other areas of the reserve, some of these are edible by humans and some are even enjoyed by foraging cattle and smaller animals such as mice supplementing their diets. Milk caps (*Lactarius*) are common along this stretch, so called because they exude a milky substance when the flesh is cut or bruised. You may spot what looks like the remains of someone's picnic, a piece of orange peel. Closer inspection will reveal an orange elf-cup fungus (*Peziza aurantia*).

Just after crossing the river the line runs under the lower slopes of Wyloer Hill. The tunnel, hand hewn from the mountain, extends for 340 metres (1,115 feet) emerging to cross the river again. The track then follows the south bank of the river, along the foot of Gamallt Hill, until the Marteg waters join those of the Wye at Marteg Bridge. The tunnel is brick faced to stop water seeping in through fissures in

SHEEP – THE MAINSTAY OF HILL FARMING.

the rock. This would freeze in the winter causing pieces of rock to shatter off, potentially landing on the line and causing an accident. At regular intervals along the tunnel are small, partially bricked alcoves which were used to store tools and to provide a retreat for workmen when a train steamed through the tunnel.

After the closure of the line, the tunnel portals were sealed up, apart from some ventilation holes. This created a stable habitat, protected from the extremes of the Welsh winter temperatures. It also meant that the tunnel remained humid and, most importantly, undisturbed. This combination of circumstances provided an ideal winter home for those much maligned mammals, bats (*Chiroptera*).

Sadly, for the bats that is, the tunnel was reopened in the 1980s to allow vehicle access for the removal of sleepers and ballast. The reopening meant that the tunnel was no longer buffered from either the extremes of temperature outside or human disturbance. Fortunately, now that it is part of the nature reserve, the tunnel has been modified to create a designer home for hibernating bats.

Gilfach tunnel is used by five species of bats: Natterer's (*Myotis nattereri*), whisk-

TAWNY OWL AND RESTORED LONGHOUSE.

ered (*M. mystacinus*), Daubenton's (*M. daubentoni*), brown long-eared (*Pleocotus auritus*) and the tiny pipistrelle (*Pipistrellus pipistrellus*), one of the smallest mammals in Britain, a mere 5g in weight and less than the length of a human thumb. It is hoped that the measures taken in the tunnel will mean that the numbers of bats hibernating here will increase over the years.

The tunnel provides a refuge (a hibernaculum) for bats in the winter. Bats' small size and low energy reserves mean that they can easily suffer from exposure. To help the bats counteract this, the tunnel entrances have been modified. The southern end of the tunnel is a bats only entrance. The bats enter and leave between metal bars which have been fixed to the tunnel mouth. The northern entrance has been almost completely bricked up apart from a small gap at the top, for the bats, and a pair of large doors allowing for human access. In the summer months, when no bats are in residence, the doors can be opened for vehicles if need be. However, during the winter months it is imperative to the bats' survival that they be disturbed as little as possible. It has been shown that a mere five visits by humans during the winter can reduce the number of bats surviving hibernation by 50%. Half a dozen such disturbances could mean a bat loses a month's fat reserves. Should spring be late or wet and insects not available, this would almost certainly be fatal.

Within the hibernaculum, the bats require places in which to while away the winter. The classic image of bats in caves (or tunnels) is of them hanging upside down from the ceiling in groups. Of the species represented at Gilfach, only whiskered and Daubenton's regularly take up this stance. Daubenton's can be found in clusters of up to a hundred individuals, sleeping away the cold days arranged next to each other like tiles on a roof. Hanging in groups reduces an individual's heat loss, the centre of the group being really quite warm. Others, such as Natterer's and long-eareds can occasionally be found hanging free, their wing membranes wrapped closely around their bodies, for all the world like Dracula and his cloak! But, like the tiny pipistrelle, they are more often to be found squeezed into small crevices either by themselves or in the company of two or three others. The number of such nooks and crannies in the tunnel has been artificially increased by opening up existing crevices in the walls, placing piles of bricks on the floor and by attaching concrete breeze blocks and pieces of timber cladding up against the wall.

Being in groups, or squeezed into small places helps reduce heat loss during hibernation, as does the lowering of the animal's metabolic rate. During hibernation bats decrease their heart rate to 25 beats a minute as compared to 500 when awake and resting and over 800 when in flight. Correspondingly, their breathing also slows and becomes quite irregular. In comparison to 550 breaths a minute during flight and nearly 200 when at rest, the hibernating bat breathes only some 30 times a minute and this can drop to less than once every 6 minutes! This all helps to minimize the energy needed to survive during hibernation, thus ensuring enough reserves of body fat to last the winter.

Hibernating bats are very sensitive to changes in temperature and each species has differing requirements that affect their choice of hibernaculum. For example, despite its size, the pipistrelle is relatively insensitive to cold and will be found hibernating within 50 metres (55 yards) of the tunnel entrance. In contrast, Daubenton's bats prefer a site with greater humidity and a higher, more stable temperature. Thus, they will roost deeper in the tunnel where they are better protected from the extremes of the weather outside.

Throughout the winter, bats will naturally rouse from their deep sleep. While it is not clear what triggers these awakenings, one theory is that it may be a full bladder! Certainly, the first thing a bat does is to urinate. The processes involved in metabolism use up water, and bats can easily dehydrate if their surroundings are not sufficiently humid. When awake, the bats will drink from any available source, including droplets formed on their fur and, if conditions are suitable, they will even feed and can occasionally be seen out hunting in the short winter day.

THE MID-WALES RAILWAY

The Mid-Wales Railway formeed one of the sections of the Cambrian Railways system of lines running throughout Wales. The part of the line running from Moat Lane Junction, near Newtown, to Talyllyn Junction near Brecon was one of the most remote. It traversed 56 miles (90 kilometres) of some of the most rugged, majestic and uninhabited scenery in Britain, reaching heights of over 330 metres (1,080 feet) above sea level.

The single-track line was served by small Cambrian 0-6-0 steam locomotives that puffed their way past fields, isolated farmhouses and open moorland. This stretch of line, running past Gilfach, was the culmination of a plan reflecting the prosperity of the Industrial Revolution. Opened in 1864, it was designed to carry cotton, imported from the Americas, from Milford Haven to the 'satanic mills' of Lancashire and to bring back goods for export. In addition it provided a means of opening up the Mid-Wales area to passengers in the age before the car. Along with passengers, it brought a wider variety of goods than had previously been obtainable in the area. Several trains a day ran, and the timetable can still be recited by some farmers through whose land they passed.

Unfortunately, the line was not as profitable as its promoters had hoped, having to compete with the bigger 'Shrewsbury and Hereford' line to the east and the 'Manchester and Milford' to the west. It was finally closed in 1962, a victim of the Beeching rationalization of the railways. Its closure had a deep effect on the locality. The car is now the only real method of transport for the local population; all goods are now brought in and out by road. But the weather in the region is not kind to tarmac and this is reflected in the fact that the County Council's greatest expenditure, after education, is on road maintenance, some 15% of the total.

Bats may also wake up if the temperature around them falls too low and they will then stir themselves and move to a more favourable site. Just waking up uses substantial reserves of body fat; moving site uses even more and, as energy reserves are at a premium, it is dangerous to stay awake for long in winter.

Some bats have evolved to make a social use of the close proximity of their

BATS IN THE BELFRY

There are fourteen species of bat in Britain, all of which are small and insectivores and most are now rare. British bats evolved to live in woodland and river valleys using caves and hollow trees as roosts. Over the centuries Britain's woodland has decreased dramatically through man's activities and bats accordingly adapted to live in buildings, tunnels and belfries. Though there are plenty of buildings about, bat populations have declined severely. For example, in the last hundred years the once common Greater Horseshoe bat population has decreased by 98%! Even within the last decade some colonies of common species have been halved. Why?

The decline of British bats has three main causes. Bad weather conditions at critical periods of the bats' life cycle, such as during the breeding season, are beyond our control. However, we can do something about the other two factors, namely loss of roosts and the loss of feeding habitats and associated insects.

Potential roosts in old railway tunnels and mines are lost when they are used as rubbish tips or the entrances are blocked for safety reasons. Preventing human entry

does not mean that access by bats should be denied. Natural roosts in old trees disappear when trees are felled or tidied. Many trees mistakenly regarded as dangerous are removed, instead of being left or secured. Trees along river banks are often cleared for reasons of pure convenience to man during the canalization of waterways.

Roost sites in buildings are rendered useless by the blocking of bat sized entrances, such as ventilators, retiling roofs and the filling of cavity walls. Just as disastrous is the widespread use of fungicides and organochlorine woodworm killers, such as lindane, in timber treatment. These chemicals are lethal to bats, and are poisonous to mammals generally. Even years after treatment, bats can die by being in contact with such surfaces. Over 10,000 buildings a year are turned into these death traps. While no-one wants woodworm, there is no longer any excuse to destroy bats as well. Synthetic pyrethroid insecticides are now available which are less toxic to bats yet effectively kill woodworm.

The second cause of bat decline is loss of habitat and

fellows in the hibernaculum. Both Daubenton's and whiskered bats will mate in winter, hanging upside down facing each other. Natterer's and long-eared bats tend to mate in the autumn and pipistrelle in late summer and early autumn. However, in all cases, fertilization is delayed until the spring. If pregnancy started during the winter, the developing young would use the mother's energy reserves

food. Habitat destruction, as in the removal of hedge-rows, canalization of rivers and pollution in general have significantly reduced the variety and quantity of night flying insects - essential food for bats. Modern farmers no longer make hay, but cut grass for silage. This is done before the plants flower and interferes with the life cycle of insects which rely on the flowers for successful maturation and breeding. Insects are also removed with pesticides, and even those that survive carry traces of the persistent chemicals which accumulate in the bat's body and cause its death.

Perhaps, as individuals, we cannot directly stop tunnels being closed or farmers using pesticides. But we can help by providing access to our homes for roosting sites or setting up bat boxes in favourable locations. Bats do not cause damage to buildings or paintwork; their droppings do not smell and dry to a fine dust. In fact, bats in your own personal belfry can be a delight to watch as they leave to hunt and provide a great talking point!

Since the enactment of the Wildlife and Countryside Act of 1981, bats are fully protected. It is illegal to handle, kill or injure a bat, to possess or sell one (live or dead), or to disturb a roosting site unless you have a licence from English Nature or its equivalent. However, you can treat an injured bat, to be released later.

It is illegal to attempt to get rid of bats by damaging roost access. Equally, the law forbids you to undertake timber treatment likely to disturb bats or their roosts without first informing the authoritative body. But, you can gently remove a bat from your living area - usually this will be a youngster that has got a bit lost.

All this may seem a bit much and rather a nuisance, but as we have seen bats are beautiful, interesting and useful creatures. Their perilous status in Britain is due to our actions. Surely, it is our responsibility and pleasure to try and rectify the situation before it is too late?

So why not become a 'BATMAN' and be a bat's friend! Further information on how can be obtained from your regional office or local bat group.

and drastically lower her, and their, chances of surviving to spring.

For all British bats the most important chore of the summer is to eat as much as they can in order to put on enough weight to last the fast approaching winter. As they are insectivores they rely heavily on good weather to ensure insects are out and about. Unfortunately, good weather is not the sole requirement. Insect populations have been drastically reduced by the destruction of natural habitats, such as hedgerows and conversion to large fields of intensive arable agriculture. It is estimated that the removal of hedgerows alone caused a 50% decrease in the numbers of insects between 1945 and 1960. The use of insecticides, and pollution in general, has further ravaged insect numbers. As well as the direct effects of food shortages, bats also have suffered poisoning by eating insects containing

THE DUSK PATROL – LONG-EARED BATS OUT HUNTING.

SURFACE SKIMMING DAUBENTON'S BATS UPSTREAM OF FFRWD FAWR.

traces of persistent pesticides. Bats eat a lot of food in proportion to their own body weight and any organochlorines ingested accumulate in their body fat. These fat stores are utilized over the hibernation period, resulting in a lethal concentration of the poisons in the bat's body by the end of the winter.

Insects, such as succulent, fatty grubs, are a nutritious food supply, as the diet of many tribal peoples testifies. However, bats hunt on the wing and take the less nutritious moths, midges and other flying prey. Substantial energy is needed when flying and a bat needs to eat about a third of its body weight every day during the summer in order to build up its winter reserves. This would be equivalent to me eating over 19 kilogrammes (41 pounds) of food every day! In numbers of insects, this represents thousands taken by each bat. It has been calculated that 100 pipistrelles (our smallest bat) will eat over 2 million gnats in a month!

The sheer number of insects taken shows bats are efficient hunters and helping them to increase their populations will only enhance their role as natural insecticides. Brown long-eared bats eat both the turnip moth (*Agrotis segetum*) and the green oak moth (*Tortrix viridana*). The former lays its eggs in the stems of turnips and the larvae burrow down into the tuber below. If you are not overly fond of turnips this may seem no bad thing, but turnips are important as winter feed for cattle, and for those of us who celebrate Burns night! The effects of green oak moth infestation can be all too clearly seen. These creatures lay their eggs in parcels of young oak leaves wrapped together while still attached to the tree. The

PLANTS WITH A PURPOSE

Homes in out-of-the-way valleys and on remote hillsides had to provide not only food and fuel, but also medicines as doctors were few and far between. Many plants had a variety of uses such as the ubiquitous nettle (*Galeopsis tetrahit*), originally a woodland plant. In spite of our childhood memories of nettle stings, this plant has been a longtime friend of man. The young leaves could be used to make a nourishing soup or an alcoholic drink, my mother can remember making nettle beer. Nettle seeds mixed with honey were used to cure colic and insomnia and the stings to ease the pain of rheumatism and muscle cramp. The stalks of older plants were harvested as a crop to make cloth until well into the 18th century when it was superceded by flax (*Linum usitatissimum*).

Lady's bedstraw (*Gallium verum*), a delicate flower found on the drier banks around Gilfach, had several uses. As its name suggests it was used to stuff mattresses and legend has it that the Virgin Mary gave birth on a mattress made of bracken and bedstraw, hence the prefix 'Lady'. The tale goes on to say that the bracken refused to recognize the Christ Child and so lost its flowers, while the bedstraw, welcoming the Child, had its flowers changed from white to gold. Legends aside, bedstraw was also used as a rennet substitute to curdle milk when making cheese, often aided by the addition of a few nettle leaves. Bedstraw roots were used to dye cloth red and the plant to make a yellow dye. Steeped in a bowl of warm water the plant had refreshing qualities as a footbath – according to a 17th-century writer it provided relief to the feet of footman and lackeys in hot weather, and, no doubt, to a few farmers as well!

feeding of the larvae of these and other insects can result in a tree being virtually denuded of its life-giving leaves.

As well as the benefit of the tunnel as a hibernaculum, Gilfach offers bats a choice of hunting habitats. The shallow waters of the Marteg, with its overhanging vegetation, tranquil pools and stretches of babbling brook, is home to a multitude of midges, moths, beetles, boatmen, caddis and dragonflies. The Natterer's, Daubenton's and whiskered bats all hunt around water. Natterer's fly with a slow, strong wing beat above water and nearby woodland, including overhanging vegetation. These bats can hover and pick up insects from leaves and branches. In contrast, whiskered bats have a weaving flight path taking them over the flowing water and adjacent pastures. Daubenton's bats also are agile in flight; their party trick is their ability to fly low over the surface of slow flowing waters, at a height of as little as 5 centimetres (2 inches)! Here they catch caddis flies and other aquatic insects. The minute pipistrelle whizzes about over open ground and along woodland edges. Its flight path is just above head height, some 2 metres (6. 5 feet) above ground. Its wings flutter rapidly and it twists and turns as it hunts, in a way to make you feel quite dizzy. The brown long-eared also twists and turns in and out of tree branches but its broad wings mean it can also fly slowly and hover while it plucks off juicy caterpillars and spiders.

Bad summer weather, with few prey, may mean the bats go hungry. Too many such nights can have severe implications. A wet or cold summer means they are less likely to have put on enough weight to survive the winter. Thus, no matter how well designed the Gilfach tunnel is as a hibernaculum, and the wide variety of habitats conserved in the reserve, there is always an element of luck involved in a bat's survival.

3

HANGING OAKS

Adding relief and a splash of deeper green to the smoothly rounded slopes behind Gilfach's farm buildings is a small sessile oakwood. This is a descendant of those ancient oakwoods that once were common throughout the country. So common that an ambitious squirrel might have travelled from Land's End to John O'Groats, passing up through Wales, without ever needing to have touched the ground! Sadly very little of our ancient woodland now remains, and daily more comes under threat from the ravages of progress. Though the previous inhabitants of this country have been clearing the forest, especially since Neolithic times, some 6,000 years ago, the rate at which we, in the late 20th century, are destroying our woodland heritage is phenomenal. In the forty years between the end of the Second World War and the mid-1980s we turned over 50% of this, perhaps our richest habitat, to the biological wasteland of concrete, tarmac, bricks, mortar, plantations and monoculture arable land.

The oakwood lies upslope of the farmhouse facing to the north. It is only a small wood, covering 25 acres (10 hectares), and somewhat unusual in that the trees are all of similar age, around fifty years old, mere teenagers as far as oak trees are concerned! The wood was clear felled (completely felled), during the First World War. There are many possible reasons why the wood was flattened. Certainly the timber would have been a useful resource for the war effort and the cleared land would have provided additional grazing for sheep — and meat was always welcome during the long years of rationing. The present woodland is not a result of replanting but of natural regeneration — a chancy business as we will see.

The oak trees at Gilfach are not those splendidly majestic trees we associate with the rich soils of lowland Britain. Those lowland cousins are *Quercus robur*, colloquially known as the common, pedunculate or English oak. The hardy specimens we see at Gilfach belong to the species *Quercus petraea* (also called *Quercus sessiliflora*). It has several common names, 'sessile' or 'durmast oak', or its somewhat more derogatory name of 'scrub oak'. These two oak species are the largest and the longest-lived of our thirty-five native trees.

Native species are those that have spread into the country with no assistance from man. In essence these are species of plants and animals which arrived in

Britain between 10,000 and 7,000 years ago, that is between the end of the last ice age and the time when Britain was cut off from mainland Europe. The water released from the melting glaciers caused the level of the seas to rise, flooding the land between Britain and the Continent and forming the North Sea and English Channel. This new body of water prevented any further colonization of Britain by plants such as trees. Native tree species include the familiar oaks, ash and birch, alder and beech (*Fagus sylvatica*). It may come as a surprise to learn that many commonly seen trees were imported by man because they were useful or ornamental. For example, the sweet chestnut (*Castanea sativa*) and sycamore (*Acer psuedoplatanus*), present in many English woods, were brought to Britain by the Romans, whilst that childhood favourite, the horse chestnut (*Aesculus hippocastanum*), with its springtime candles and autumnal provision of conkers, did not arrive in the country until the 16th century when it was imported from its native Greece to grace British parklands.

There are some differences between the two oaks, reflected in their names. In profile, the sessile oak is narrower than its lowland cousin, and, though both can grow to a height of 30 metres (98 feet), the sessile oak tends to be smaller, stunted and often twisted in form, hence its name of scrub oak. Certainly those we see at Gilfach are still quite small, partly because of their youth but also because of the relative impoverishment of the soil in which they grow. The soils are quite acidic, with a pH between 3.5 and 5, and light. The steepness of the slope helps drain these soils — a condition which promotes rapid leaching away of the nutrients. The sessile oak is far more tolerant of such infertile conditions than its cousin. The lack of nutrients is just one factor causing the stunted growth typical of upland sessile oakwoods. Another important factor is wind. The constant force of the wind causes young trees to grow at an angle. They grow bending away from the direction of the prevailing wind, leaving the impression that the trees are clinging grimly to the mountainside — indeed such woods are often known as hanging oakwoods.

The word 'sessile' means sedentary, particularly when talking about animals such as barnacles who remain virtually fixed to one spot throughout their adult lives. In the case of the sessile oak, it means 'unstalked' and refers to the acorns. The acorns of the English oak grow on long stalks called 'peduncles' — hence the name pedunculate oak. In contrast, those of the sessile oak have no such stalk. The acorn cup grows straight from the twig, appearing to be sitting on it.

The crown of an individual oak tree is fan-shaped, rising above the boughless trunk. The branches have a characteristic zig-zag appearance, especially notice-able in winter when they are bare of leaves. The zig-zag is due to the leading shoot on the end of a twig failing to grow, perhaps because of exposure to the wind, and a stronger side shoot then continuing the last year's growth, hence the jointed appearance of the trees.

The bark of the oak is another characteristic feature. It is rough and deeply fissured, providing homes for a myriad of small creatures. From the tree's point of view the bark is essential and, as man soon discovered, cutting the bark right round its circumference will cause any tree to die. The bark acts like a thick overcoat, protecting the tree from the extremes of weather and from attack from enemies large and small, bacteria and fungi, rabbits and sheep. When food is scarce, such as in a particularly hard winter, animals like deer may destroy so much of the bark that the top of a tree dies. Whilst the main branches fan out from the top of the trunk, you may notice short shoots growing on the trunk. These potentially are very important as they can grow into new branches if the crown of the tree should die back, or be cut back.

The bark comprises two layers, a living inner layer and a dead outer layer. The inner layer, or phloem, is a vital part of the tree's transport system, carrying nourishing sug-ars down from the leaves where they are manufactured to the roots below. The bark is formed from a layer of special cells known as 'bark cambium'. This green, living tissue produces the corky cells we see on the out-side of the tree. The colour change from green to browny-grey is due to the laying down of waterproof waxes in the cell walls. These waxes act as a mackintosh keeping excess water out of the tree. They also play an equally important role during dry, warm periods by preventing moisture escaping from the tree. The combination of the

NATTERER'S BAT.

WEASEL – GETTING A BETTER VIEW.

cambium and corky cells is known as the periderm. In the majority of tree species this first layer of periderm is followed by others originating in progressively deeper layers of the stem. With the formation of each new periderm, the one preceding it is cut off from its source of nutrients and water and thus dies, forming the dead bark layer we associate with tree trunks and branches. It is startling to realize that some 90% of a tree comprises dead matter!

As the branches and trunk grow so they increase in girth. A plant which increases in size, height and girth, year on year is known as a single-stemmed, woody perennial. Oak is also known as a broadleaved tree, a term describing the shape of its leaves compared to the narrow needle-shaped leaves of conifers. Most broadleaved trees are deciduous, that is they lose their leaves every winter, an exception being the holly. In deciduous trees, growth is seasonal. It is very rapid in spring, slowing down through the summer and autumn and stopping altogether in winter, the cycle re-commencing the following spring. This pattern of growth-no growth is reflected in the tree's wood by rings of light and dark cells. The light rings indicate the period of growth, so the wider the light coloured ring the better was the spring and summer for growing that year. It is these rings which form the grain of the wood, so beautiful when polished.

Counting tree rings goes under the technical term of 'dendro-chronology' (literally tree-timing). It is an important technique used by archaeologists and biologists. It can be used for dating human and biological features. By knowing when a piece of wood was cut you can work backwards to know just how old it was and thus roughly date objects found around it. Thankfully, dendro-chronologists do not have to cut down trees to work out their age. Instead they use a special tool to extract a core from the whole depth of the trunk, right down to the heartwood and then they may count the rings. They then replace the core and seal the wound with non-toxic wax to keep out any infection. But if you wish to indulge in ageing trees there is an easier way, perhaps not quite so accurate but having the advantage of being totally harmless to the tree. As the tree grows so does the circumference of the trunk and this fact can be used as a measuring tool. If you measure the girth of the oak tree trunk at about a height of 1.5 metres (4.5 feet), this will give you the age in years if you measure in inches; divide by 2.5 if you measured in centimetres.

Oak trees are the grand old men of the British countryside, living longer than any other native species. They can live for up to 800 years, though 300 is probably nearer the average. All being well, the youngsters you now see at Gilfach will be around in the year 2500, halfway through the next millennium. The great ages attained by oak trees span many human generations and have been a major reason for the reverence man has bestowed on them. They formed an integral part of the ancient religion of the Druids and have often been part of local folklore. Indeed, in 1670 one John Smith, a respected forestry expert of his time, maintained that some of the oaks then alive dated back to the first summer after Noah's flood and a few went back as far as creation. I think his knowledge of dendro-chronology was a little primitive.

A JAY SURVEYS THE SNOW-COVERED GILFACH OAKWOOD.

Because oaks are so long-lived it is difficult to notice any changes in an oak tree population, that is the number of trees in any particular woodland, unless extremely accurate records are maintained for many decades … which is unlikely. Oakwood is the climax vegetation over much of Britain, and certainly so in this part of Wales. What this means is that had there been no other interference, from man, for example, then oakwood would have been the culmination of a succession of plant communities competing for the same piece of land. This succession would have started with lichens, progressed through a herb and grass community, birch and hazel woods, until finally the area would have been dominated by oakwood. When a particular species of tree dominates a woodland community, it is usually because the root system of that species is so effective at collecting water and nutrients from the soil that it enables the plant to grow tall enough to shade out other competing species. The sessile oak is one such dominant species and its successful adaptation to the environmental conditions of upland Britain indicates that there is no foreseeable change to the nature of woodlands here; unless there is a significant climatic change such as another ice age! A climax community, such as a sessile oakwood, therefore is regarded as a 'stable ecosystem'. An 'ecosystem' is a dynamic community of plants and animals, living within a framework of rocks, soils and weather.

It may be assumed that such a successful climax community would be able to recover quite easily from any disturbance. But this is not the case. The sessile oak is known as a 'k-strategy species', as indeed is man. The term, 'k-strategy', refers to several characteristics to do with an organism's lifecycle and, in particular, how it reproduces itself under natural conditions. As with man, the oak is large, grows slowly and lives a long time. It is rarely killed by the attacks of other species, having invested heavily in defence systems, such as its thick, fissured bark. Other features of a k-strategist include a low population replacement rate, which means that the population does not increase very fast and the number of individuals per unit area tends to remain roughly the same from one generation to another. All this adds up to an inability to recover quickly from any substantial disturbance, such as the wood being clear felled by man, as happened here at Gilfach.

'From the tiny acorn the mighty oak doth grow', and anyone walking through the woods in autumn will know that there are plenty of acorns around and each one has the potential to grow into a mature tree and produce its own acorn offspring. In fact in a good year a single mature oak tree (say between 100 and 200 years old) can produce 50,000 acorns, though it is estimated that 30,000 is more normal. So during an average reproductive life of a couple of centuries, a single oak tree could produce an incredible 6 million acorns, and it only needs one to grow up and replace the parent tree when it dies! So why the inability of the oakwood to recover easily from major disturbances? Well, to put it bluntly, very few acorns ever survive to reach maturity. Acorns are heavy objects and do not get dispersed by wind, unlike seeds from other species such as dandelion (*Taraxacum officinale*) or sycamore. Rather, the oak depends on animals to transport the acorns to suitable growing sites. Jays (*Garrulus glandarius*) collect acorns as food, carrying them away to eat them undisturbed, or to bury them in open ground often stashing away enough to last all through the winter. Squirrels (*Sciurus*) too collect acorns and bury them in the woodland soil, storing them away to be consumed during the cold winter months. Not all are rediscovered or needed as winter food and these have the chance of germinating in the following spring, appearing above the earth as tiny seedlings. In order to attract such animals, the oak must produce enough acorns to be able to afford to lose most as food for the squirrels and jays. Other acorns will remain where they landed below the parent tree and be nibbled by smaller woodland creatures such as woodmice (*Apodemus sylvaticus*), or merely rot in the damp autumnal weather.

WAX CAP FUNGUS.

Even those acorns that manage to germinate still have many obstacles to face before they grow up. The young plant may be shaded out by larger trees around it and not receive enough sunlight to enable it to grow. Or, as with the seed in the parable, the acorn may have landed on stony ground and only have enough soil to support a few years growth, eventually starving to death or only growing to a small size. One such oak can be seen growing in a cleft of rock on Wyloer Hill. The tender young shoots are very palatable and may be eaten by rabbits or sheep, but this tree was protected by the rock from being grazed. Its low branching shape at the point where it is no longer protected suggest that the growing tip was grazed out by sheep. Indeed, this susceptibility to being grazed is a major reason why the trees at Gilfach are all of similar age. Presumably when they were first growing they were protected from being eaten. After a few years, however, and until the site was bought by the nature trust, the wood had been used for grazing sheep and any younger seedlings would not have survived. In its new existence, the wood will be completely fenced off from the sheep, allowing trees of various ages to grow, resulting in a more natural scenario. Life as a young oak is a bit of a gamble and it is not easy to become a mature oak tree; those we see at Gilfach are the lucky few who have made it, at least to the stage of being young adults. For remember, an oak is not really considered mature, until it produces its first crop of acorns, at around sixty years old or more!

One way in which an acorn is given a chance of reaching maturity, is when an adult tree is blown over in the wind, or when a dead tree finally falls over. What happens then is a microcosm of what happens on a larger scale when mass felling occurs. If you stand in the Gilfach oakwood, or any other oakwood, and look up, you will see that the roof of the wood is a mass of oak tree canopies, yet there is still a lot of light down where you are standing. This is in direct contrast to the darkness of conifer woods and is because the oak trees naturally grow far enough away from each other that the canopies barely touch, requiring greater acrobatic feats from the resident squirrels. As we will see later, this open canopy means that plants and animals of many species can live on the woodland floor. When an adult tree falls even more light can penetrate to the ground through the resulting 'light chimney'. Such a chimney provides a small open habitat, a miniature glade or clearing. For a short time, a period of 2 or 3 years, this clearing is open to colonization from a wide variety of plants, and their attendant animal species. These colonizing species are known as opportunists; many of these plants arrive as tiny seeds, borne on the wind to a new, suitable habitat. The seeds from the dominant trees – in the case of Gilfach, acorns – soon germinate and become successfully started in their long years of growth. Unlike the colonizing plants, which are annuals, the oak seedlings do not die back every year. Rather, their perennial type of growth means that each year they get larger and larger and soon start to out-compete and shade out the other species, finally rendering the woodland an almost closed, self-sustaining, stable community again. Part of the management of the Gilfach oakwood will include the deliberate felling of some trees to create light chimneys and glades, thus promoting the growth of a new generation; to promote a wide range of species, there needs to be a wide range of ages of trees.

The oak tree itself can be considered as an ecosystem in its own right, providing a total, or partial, life support system for a myriad of creatures. During a lifespan of some 300 years a single oak tree may be inhabited by at least 284 different species. Many of these are parasites, and the oak is subject to many diseases and parasites, though it does not suffer them all simultaneously. Like us really. We too act as hosts to many forms of bacteria and tiny mites which we hardly consider. We are aware of others (such as the fungus causing athlete's foot), but they are unlikely to cause death. Indeed, it is not in a parasite's interest to destroy its host and thus its livelihood. The oak tree has been part of Britain's landscape for many thousands of years and is well adjusted to the climate and soils. This means that it is able to withstand mass attacks by a variety of insects and fungi. Not all, however. Honey or boot-lace fungus (*Armillaria mellea*) is perhaps the most dangerous enemy of the tree (next to man, of course). This fungus causes root rot, which eventually kills the tree. It spreads from tree to tree through the soil by means of long shoestring-like structures called 'rhizomorphs'. It also grows up through the tree and wood containing this fungus is luminous in the dark, emitting a ghostly light from freshly cut logs.

A young seedling oak, struggling to grow up towards the light, may be attacked by one of the weevil species. These beetles form a family of 500 different species called *Curculionidae*. They have a hard outer covering which provides some protection against predators and against excessive loss of moisture, in the same way as the oak's bark. The head of a weevil is drawn out into a pointed snout which contains a pair of tiny, but tough, jaws. Some weevils eat into the soft bark of the seedling oak's main shoot, its young trunk, where they mate and lay their eggs. These eggs hatch into larvae which make their way down into the soil and feast on the roots of the young tree. As the larvae also have other soil-based food supplies, the seedling will usually survive such an attack. Others, such as the red oak roller weevil (*Attelabus nitens*), have a predilection for the tender leaves of young trees and are rarely found on mature oaks. If you wander through the Gilfach oakwood in the month of May you may spot these brightly coloured creatures. The female is about 6 millimetres (0.25 inches) long, and her bright red colour acts as a warning to potential predators, perhaps that these weevils aren't very tasty. She lays a single egg on the upper side of a leaf and then carefully cuts a slit on each side of the leaf towards the midrib. Then, like a genii rolling up his magic carpet, she rolls the cut portions of the leaf into a tunnel, providing a sheltered nursery for the egg and the larva when it hatches. Her final gesture of maternal care is to bite part way into the leaf stalk, cutting it off from its supply of nutrients and water. This in turn means that the leaf turns brown, withers and drops, but not before the larva has eaten the inner part of the roll and turned into a pupa. The pupa will then hatch into an adult weevil, find a mate the following spring and rear its own youngsters.

Oak leaves of both young and mature trees are the staple food of many insect larvae: they are bitten and chewed by adult weevils and the caterpillars of butterflies; they are sucked of their nutritious juices by bugs and mined by moth caterpillars who leave distinctive wiggly tracks in the leaf surface. They can be disfigured, sometimes grotesquely, by the formation of galls resulting from attack by a variety of midges, wasps and mites. These tiny creatures lay their eggs in the living tissue of the leaf. The eggs act as an irritant causing that part of the leaf to swell, producing new healing tissue and thus creating a home for the larvae. Galls may be hard and green as in the marble gall or light brown and spongy as oak apples, caused by the ministrations of the gall wasps such as *Andricus kollari* and *Biorhiza pallida*. Galls can often be seen on the oak's flowers and twigs as well.

Not only are the leaves subject to attack by a great diversity of insects, but the number of any one species present can be phenomenal. In some years the canopy of a single large oak can play host to 250,000 caterpillars of the winter moth (*Operophytera brumata*), along with a multitude of larvae from other species, including the notorious green oak moths. The adult winter moth emerges from its pupa, which has been lying in the soil, during November and December. The female is

HOLY OAK

Trees have always been important to us, providing for our physical needs as sources of timber, firewood and food. Yet at the same time forests and woods have been wild and hostile, the home of animals, not men. Indeed, the word 'savage' (originally 'salvage') is derived from the Latin word '*silva*' meaning wood. It was not just animals and ferocious beasts who lived in the wildwood, so did gods and spirits, some kindly, some downright evil! Throughout the world trees have been worshipped as gods themselves or the dwelling places of gods and spirits, and Wales was no exception.

We should remember that for much of our history, certainly into the early modern period (1500-1800) life was fraught with dangers from disease, poverty and wild animals. Bears, wild boar and wolves were not creatures met only in fairy stories, they were there in the flesh, lurking in the woods and threatening village folk and those who earned their livings from the forest. In fact, the last wolf in Wales was killed some twenty miles from Gilfach in the late 1500s. It is not surprising then that such inhospitable places should be the homes of 'higher beings', namely gods and spirits.

The Celts have left few written records, but we know they believed in many gods, a pantheistic religion. The Druids acted as intermediaries between the spirit and mortal worlds. They ascribed deities to certain physical features like springs, hill tops and, in particular, sacred trees. For them the heart of the forest was the seat of the godhead in sanctuaries of dark groves and dimly lit woodland clearings. From the writings of Roman observers such as Pliny and Strabo, we know that it was in such clearings that the Celts believed the Green Man ruled, Kernnunos, the consort of the Goddess. Strabo noted that one of the key words used by Celts when referring to their religious ritual was '*nemeton*', translated as 'sacred place'. He specifically refers to the meeting place of a council of Druids as '*drunemeton*', or 'sanctuary of the oaks'.

The Celtic word for oak is '*duir*', also written as '*dwr*' or '*derw*', and it is likely that the word Druid is derived from this. The Druidic year was based on the cycles of the moon and contained thirteen lunar months. The seventh month, falling in the middle of the year, was the month of the oak, corresponding to the modern month of May. It was preceded by the 'month of conception' symbolized by the hawthorn tree and followed by the month of the holly. The oak tree and its leaves represented fertility, primeval strength, solid protection and the ability to survive and overcome. It was also the doorway to mystery, especially if the tree was found to bear mistletoe. Mistletoe is a semi–parasitic plant which buries its roots into the oak's bark and taps the nutritious sap from it. In November and early December it produces sticky white berries, the juice of which was used by Druidic priests to induce a hallucinatory state – enabling them to mediate between man and the spirit world.

The oak and the holly had a deeper meaning for people. The mighty oak at the height of its annual season

wingless and must make the long vertical climb up the trunk to lay her eggs in crevices in the upper twigs of the trees, a notable feat. The males can fly and, by releasing a special scent (pheromone), the female attracts prospective mates from a mile or more away. The eggs hatch in mid-April and the larvae then climb along the twig and enter a leaf bud. Between then and June these caterpillars feast on the young leaves and, when numerous, these tiny creatures can totally defoliate the tree. In June the fully fed larvae spin a thread of silk and lower themselves to the ground where they pupate in the soil. In years of a bad attack, the tree may produce a second flush of leaves, known as the Lammas growth (Lammas being the name of an old Anglo-Saxon church festival held on the first of August when the first fruits of the harvest were offered).

The oak of course is not prone to such a massive, debilitating attack in most

---

is wreathed in leaves and bears thousands of acorns, all of which are lost in the winds of autumn. In contrast, the evergreen holly with its sprigs of bright red berries proclaims 'life in death' in the midst of winter. It is no accident that in the famous Celtic Arthurian legend of Sir Gawaine and the Green Knight, the two protagonists are often represented by the oak and the holly.

Although the natural clearings may have been transformed to wood, and then stone henges, such as at Avebury and Stonehenge, their forest origins are clear. Indeed, a similar reference can be seen in medieval churches – the tree–like columns with highly stylized canopy tops. The early Christians in Britain had to convert people from the old religion to the new and, as with later missionaries, they found it easier to incorporate elements of the earlier religion. The importance of trees was no exception. In many medieval churches, close examination of the roof bosses and under the misericordes will reveal carvings of oak leaves and acorns – hidden tributes to the old gods. Indeed, much later the relationship remained as in the carol 'the holly and the ivy' and in many hymns where the Cross, made of dead wood, is referred to as the tree, for example in the line written in the late 1600s:

Yea, the very nails which nail Him,
Nail us also to the Tree

Indeed, many early Protestants were adamant in their view that prayers could be as effectively said in woods as in churches. In many parishes, the annual ritual walk around the parish boundary went from one tree to another, stopping to read the scriptures at each tree demarcated as the 'gospel oak' or 'holy oak', a practice commemorated in many modern place names, such as Gospel Oak in north London.

Whilst nowadays trees are no longer usually considered in a religious context, they are held in high regard. Individual specimens are often considered as having local or national importance, such as the oak in the New Forest off which glanced the arrow that killed William Rufus, or The Martyrs' Tree at Tolpuddle, the maintenance of which is in part financed by the TUC (Trades Union Congress).

The longevity of trees, and in particular oaks, is a symbol of eternity. Trees were often planted by people who could not afford a gravestone, or to mark the birth of a child. The act of felling a tree was often used as a way of symbolically hitting someone, or worse. It was common for those with grievances against the aristocracy in the 17th century to cut down the offender's prized trees. And even today the proposed felling of trees or their loss through natural causes, as in the hurricanes of 1987, is a proper and accepted cause for outcry, lament and strivings to protect them.

years and has good defence systems. Oak leaves contain quantities of tannin and other toxic compounds which make the leaves harder to digest. However, young leaves do not contain any tannin and thus are susceptible to attack. As the year progresses so the level of tannin increases and by September up to 5% of the dry weight of an oak leaf is tannin. Tannins slow down the rate at which insect larvae grow and thus the caterpillars must have completed feeding and be ready to pupate before the tannins are laid down in any appreciable quantity.

During a wet summer you may notice that the leaves of the oak look as if someone has dusted them with talcum powder. In fact this whitish appearance is caused by the spore or fruit producing parts of a fungus known as the oak mildew fungus. The spores are spread by the wind and when they land on a leaf they develop thin threads known as 'hyphae', the fungus equivalent of roots. These invade the living leaf and draw the fungus' food from the leaf's supply of nutrients.

The leaves are the manufacturing part of the plant, little factories that take carbon dioxide from the air and energy from the sunlight. They are also fed water from the roots, which is transported up the cambium layer of the bark. From these two compounds, water and carbon dioxide, fuelled by sunlight, the leaves photosynthesize, or manufacture the sugars essential for the tree's growth. All green plants are able to perform this action, from the tiny mosses to the mighty oak. A by-product of this process is that the plant produces oxygen which it gives back to the atmosphere, and which we in turn breathe. Plants too use oxygen, but during daylight hours they give out more oxygen than they 'breathe' in and this photosynthesis process uses up carbon dioxide produced by animals such as ourselves. However, they cannot photosynthesize at night and so only use oxygen, hence the once held belief that plants should not be allowed in hospital rooms at night. The net result of the process is that they donate oxygen and use up carbon dioxide. The truth is that, without this amazing process of photosynthesis performed by green plants, the level of oxygen in the world would diminish as we animals kept using it up and not replacing it. That is one reason why so many people are concerned about the wholesale destruction of the forests of the world and refer to them as the 'lungs of the earth'. That is exactly what they are.

The trunk of the tree provides structural support to the branches and leaves and also transports water up to the leaves and sugars down from them. The outer covering of the trunk, the bark, is home to many species of insect and plant. It is only in recent centuries with the increase in atmospheric pollution that the bark of trees has been so visible. A rich and prosperous collection of lichens densely covering the barks used to be a common sight, now restricted to older trees in the relatively pollution-free woods of the west. Trees continually shed bits of bark and the bark itself is fairly dry, not a particularly hospitable environment to these beautiful, flowerless lichens. But many species have evolved to cope with living on a tree trunk and there are benefits to such a home. Most notably there is less competition from other plants, in particular flowering plants, than on the woodland floor. The deep fissures and slow growth of the bark of old oak trees give these plants an opportunity to get well entrenched and such trunks can be festooned with plant life. At Gilfach, even though the trees are still relatively young, there is a wide variety of plants growing on them in a wonderful array of greens and greys.

These plants that live on trunks and branches are known as 'epiphytes'. Unlike most plants, which gain their food and water from the soil, epiphytes absorb gases, water and nutrients from the humid air around them. They are thus more common in the west of Britain where the air tends to be saturated with water vapour from rain or mist. The absorption of substances from the air also makes these plants especially vulnerable to atmospheric pollution. Pollutants to which they are particularly sensitive include sulphur dioxide and carbon monoxide (produced when coal, oil, petrol and even smokeless fuels are burnt).

Liverworts and mosses form mats of green on the damper bark at the base of the tree. Higher up the trunk and on the branches, where the air is drier, cushion mosses can be found. These mosses have tiny upright stems protruding from the main cushion and you may have seen them growing on old walls. The upright stems trap water in the pile for the moss's use and keep the trunk surface underneath quite dry. This ability to trap water and nutrients means that mosses can provide a better substrate (growing surface) than the poor, acidic upland soils for the germination of seeds of other plants. Thus plants such as the burnet saxifrage (*Pimpinella saxifraga*) may be found growing in, or rather on, a clump of moss.

You may notice that mosses are not evenly distributed around the tree; they tend to grow best on the shaded northern side of a tree where they are less likely to dry out. (A handy thing to remember if you get lost in a wood.)For the same reason, they tend to grow better on the leeward side, sheltered from the drying effects of the prevailing wind.

The surfaces of the trunk, branches and twigs are clothed in lichen colonies, a rich tapestry of colours and textures. Like the mosses, lichens need light in order to grow. However, lichens are less vulnerable to drying out as the outer layer of fungus protects the more fragile algal member of this partnership and thus can be found making the most of the sunny, south-west aspects of trunks and branches. So the mosses and lichens are not in competition for the trunk but have adapted to different micro-habitats (tiny habitats) on the tree surface.

Lichens form a very diverse group, or genus. There are over 1,350 species just in Britain. Almost a quarter of these have been found growing on oak trees in central Wales. Each species has its own preference for a distinctive micro-habitat of the bark. For example, some prefer the deeper fissures formed by the barks of trees older than the mere striplings growing at Gilfach. Mind you, don't feel discouraged, a Gilfach lichen-spotting venture will produce a hundred or more distinct species. Lichens colonize surfaces from a central point and expand along a curved growth front, giving the basic circular form. As the growth edge advances it leaves a dying core behind. This appears as if the centre of the lichen is flaking and drying up and you may think the whole plant is dying.

Whilst I have just said that the basic shape of a lichen is circular, this must not be taken too literally. Lichens come in a baffling array of shapes — or so it seems at first. In fact they can be divided into three basic forms, with rather exotic names. Most of the lichens you will see come under the term 'crustose', namely encrusting the surface on which they are growing. They are very flat, appearing pressed or sprayed onto the tree bark. They are usually grey-green in colour with a crazy-paving, cracked appearance. These apparent cracks are often darker lines formed by the line of spore bodies.

The second group are known as 'foliose' lichens. Foliose simply means 'having leaves'. These festoon branches and tree stumps with their array of bizarre looking outgrowths. They look a bit as if someone had spent time sticking fragments of leaves onto the bark. They may form circular patches, often quite small, others may have leafy-lobes resembling diminutive cabbages. The lobes may be branched and some may have cup-like ends which are the fruiting, or spore-producing parts of the plant. In colour these foliose lichens may be a pale grey green or even browny-green.

The final group is a shrubby form called 'fructicose'. They may grow upright or hang down like tassels. They are tufted and have many tiny branches and are sometimes called 'beard lichens' for obvious reasons. Various species such as the *Usnea* family are particularly good indicators of clean air as they do not survive where there is more than 5 microgrammes of sulphur dioxide per cubic metre of

GREATER SPOTTED WOODPECKER.

air. It is nice to know that all twelve species of *Usnea* are found on oaks in central Wales – Welsh air must be good for you.

The surface of the bark provides a home for many species of flora and fauna, but the bark of trees can often suffer damage. Such damage can result in the formation of two types of hole, wet rot holes and dry rot holes. Rot holes are caused by natural damage from lightning, high winds or the behaviour of animals such as the woodpecker (*Dendrocopos*). Man's activities such as pruning, coppicing or even that long established habit of carving initials in tree trunks can also initiate the formation of rot holes. The wound in the bark means that the underlying living layer of sapwood and even the heartwood of the tree is exposed to attack from a variety of fungi. The spread of the fungi is helped along by the burrowing activities of beetles and between them they extend the damage and a cavity forms – a rot hole. Some holes occur in sheltered parts of the tree and stay dry even in a heavy rainstorm. Others are more exposed and fill with rainwater, either directly or as it runs down the branches and trunk. In these wet rot holes the water may drain away through the rotting wood or it may accumulate, especially if a layer of rotting leaves acts as a plug at the bottom of the cavity. Often the tree will form a scar or callous around the hole opening. This causes the opening to decrease, sometimes closing it altogether, even though the cavity continues to grow as the wood beneath rots away. This in turn may mean the hole does not get so water filled as less can enter, but this may be offset by the fact that the restricted opening means that any water in the hole is less likely to evaporate away.

Another form of hole, called a pan, can be formed by distorted growth of the trunk or branch due to overcrowding. These holes differ from rot holes in that the bark is not broken or damaged and the pan is more of a depression in the bark. Pans can fill with water but, because they are usually quite shallow, they soon dry in warm weather. Both rot holes and pans, especially the former, are homes to many species, some very specialized to this unique type of miniature habitat.

Wet holes are home to many tiny, microscopic creatures known as 'protozoans', including the attractively named 'slipper animalcule' or *Paramecium*, as well as tiny *Cyclops* crustacea, relatives of lobsters. Such species are commonly found in any accumulation of water, others are specifically associated with wet tree holes, for at least part of their lifecycles. This specialization means that they are restricted in their choice of home, but have the advantage of escaping their natural enemies such as predatory beetles and dragonfly (*Odonata*) larvae which do not live in such places.

One such group of specialists are the mosquitoes (*Culicidae*). In Britain there are thirty-three species of mosquito, three of which rely exclusively on tree holes in which to lay their eggs. In particular, *Orthopodomyia pulchripalpis* (a tiny creature with a very long name), prefers holes containing water darkly rich in tannin, as is found in oak trees. During the warm summer months, the female lays her eggs in the tree hole water, where either the larvae hatch almost immediately or lie dormant until the following spring. The larvae are known as wrigglers, which is an accurate description of how they move. The larva spends its time eating algae and bacteria on the cavity sides and particles of organic matter suspended in the water. As it needs air to breathe, it surfaces regularly, breathing in through an opening at the end of its body, not its mouth. As it grows, it sheds its hard outer casing, passing through four such larval stages before the pupal phase. In this stage of life it is called a 'tumbler', again a description of how it moves, and though it still surfaces to breathe, it stops eating. In the summer it emerges from the pupa as an adult mosquito, leaving its watery home to mate and feed – often on the unwary human.

Other creatures using wet holes include the notorious biting midge (*Dasyhelea dufouri*) and its non-biting cousin (*Metriocnemus martinii*) – nothing to do with the drink of the same name – and the hover-fly (*Myiatropa florea*). Only one of the hundreds of species of British beetle breeds in holes. Known as *Prionocyphon serricornis*,

WILDWOODS?

Ecologists distinguish between wildwood, ancient woodland and secondary woodland. Wildwood is woodland that has not been interfered with by man. In Britain, it is unlikely that there is any area of wildwood left. Wildwood and early man during his hunter-gatherer period managed to co-exist. But, once man had become an agriculturalist, the wildwood began to disappear through his extensive deforestation activities and his wood management techniques.

Woods that are cleared and subsequently abandoned will turn initially into heathland or grassland. However, over time, through the process of succession, the land will revert to woods again. This 'new' wood is known as secondary woodland, and is what we see at Gilfach oakwood. Ancient woodland is either wildwood which has been managed by man, such as the New Forest, or plantation or secondary woodland which has been on the site continuously since the 16th century.

Man has managed woods for many thousands of years and the traditional methods used were common well into this century and have seen a recent renaissance in the conservation management of some British woods. There were two methods of management: coppicing – the creation of woodland where the wood was used to provide crops of timber and underwood – and pollarding – the creation of wood pasture where the harvesting of a wood crop and the provision of grazing were combined. More recently, since the 17th century, plantations where trees are grown to be felled in rotation have been the predominant method of management. Though well established, this is not technically considered a traditional management system.

As we know, a natural wood is a virtually closed system consisting of a four-tiered structure rising from ground level to a height of some 30 metres (98 feet). Traditional management techniques have modified this ecosystem in a variety of ways. The major difference between a coppiced and a pollarded wood is the height at which the trees are cut. In a coppice, they are cut at ground level or just above, while pollarded trees are cut 2-4.5 metres (6.5-15 feet) above the ground, out of reach of grazing animals. An easy indicator of past coppicing in a wood is the presence of 'many-trunked' trees growing from the old coppiced stumps, or stools. In contrast, trees which were once pollarded tend to have single trunks with a low bushy crown. Pollarding is often to be seen on trees lining the streets of our major cities. The effect of both coppicing and pollarding on an

COPPICED (LEFT) VERSUS POLLARDED.

individual tree is to increase its lifespan. The remaining stump sends up new shoots, which grow about 2 metres (6.5 feet) high in the first year and then begin to thicken. These provide a crop of poles which can be harvested any time between 5 and 25 years later, depending on the size of pole you desire.

Some coppiced woods were composed purely of coppiced trees; others were coppice with standards, the latter probably being the more common form of management. Standards were trees scattered through the wood and allowed to grow unhindered until they were between 70 and 150 years old, when they were felled for their timber. The coppiced trees were of a variety of species producing crops of underwood for firewood and light construction. Standards were nearly always of oak or ash. Oak trees were often preferred as their branches corkscrew slightly as they grow, a characteristic which gives them extra strength — useful when building homes or ships.

Coppices were worked on a rotation system along the following lines. Consider a coppice wood of 100 acres (40.5 hectares) containing 5,000 coppiced stools and 2000 standards worked on a 10-year cycle. Thus each 10 acres (4 hectares) would contain around 500 stools and 200 standards. Each year, a 10-acre(4 hectare) plot would be managed by felling the coppices and 20 of the standards. Fifty self-sown seedlings or coppice poles would be left standing, a process known as singling, on the assumption that 20 of these would survive to reach timber size and so replace those taken. The following year another 10-acre plot would be harvested, and thus over the 10-year cycle the whole 100 acres would be reaped as a renewable source and the cycle would begin again.

In a coppice wood, because the stools were at or near ground level, it was important that animals were excluded at least for the first few years. Tender new shoots are very attractive to grazing animals, like sheep, deer and rabbits, and would not survive such gastronomic attention. This exclusion of animals had two effects. First it meant that the undergrowth was not disturbed and the herb and ground layer was able to continue to provide a habitat for a rich variety of plant and animal species, similar to that in the original wildwood. The second effect was that the ground was not fertilized by the faeces of the sheep. This, combined with the cyclical cropping and removal of the wood, meant there was an overall loss of stored energy and nutrients from the system. In contrast, in a pollarded wood pasture, the height at which the trees were cut meant that grazing animals could be present all the time. Whilst the dung

from these animals reduced the overall losses from the wood's ecosystem, the permanent grazing meant that the herb and shrub layers were kept at a minimum and the ground would be covered in a grassy sward containing only a few plant species.

For two or three years after coppicing there would be a dramatic increase in the level of light reaching the ground, an extensive, man-made light chimney. This encouraged the flowering of wild flowers and the proliferation of their associated butterflies, bees, beetles and other insects. Within five years the coppice shoots would have grown sufficiently to have formed a deep, impenetrable shrub layer and the flowers beneath would begin to die out. However, this increased cover would be attractive to a variety of small birds such as warblers (*Sylviidae*), thrushes (*Turdidae*) and nightingales (*Luscinia megarhyncha*). During the last five years of the cycle, the coppice shrubs would turn into a dense mass of poles unsuitable for these birds, but soon ready to be harvested. In our imaginary coppice wood, conducted on a rotation system, mobile species such as birds would move around the whole 100 acres(40.5 hectares) following the harvest rotation. Sedentary species, such as the flowering plants, would have seeds lying dormant in the ground, until conditions were again suitable to stimulate their germination.

The lack of a high canopy layer, apart from the standard trees, meant that such managed woods were not very attractive to raptors (birds of prey) and other high-nesting birds. In addition, the regular removal of the underwood meant that the ground layer was more exposed, than in the wildwood, to rainfall and thus to leaching and the loss of soil and nutrients. This was also true of pollarded wood pastures, though here the more resilient grass sward would ameliorate the effects of leaching. The grass roots would bind the soil and the grass itself act as a protective overcoat. However, the dominance of grass and the concurrent grazing meant that there was less alteration in the ground layer when the crop was harvested. Otherwise the process of succession taking place in a wood pasture would have been similar to that in a coppice.

One feature that distinguished the natural wildwood from both coppiced woods and those managed as pollarded wood pasture was that it contained dead trees. No dead trees meant no habitat for decomposer species or those birds and animals that use such dead wood as a food or nesting resource. As we have seen, decomposed dead wood is an essential part of the process of returning nutrients and energy back to the woodland ecosystem. In such managed woods, therefore, the overall fertility of the

PIED
FLYCATCHER.

ground was steadily reduced as nutrients and energy were harvested and removed as poles, timber, or, in the case of wood pasture, livestock products such as wool and meat.

The standards would be used as timbers for the building of homes and ships. Larger poles would be used for light construction and small ones as brushwood. Poles the thickness of a man's wrist were turned into charcoal, with the charcoal makers living in the forest. Oak makes excellent charcoal and the charcoal was used to separate iron from ore as early as 500 BC. As iron implements became more common, so the huge quantities of oak needed exceeded supply, simply because it is such a slow growing tree. This was exacerbated by the requirements of large timbers for building and especially for equipping the navy with ships. By the 17th century vast tracts of countryside had been robbed of their oak trees and coppicing was practised on a massive scale.

Oak bark contains harvestable quantities of tannin. The quality of the tannin decreases as the tree gets older; so if you wanted to harvest tannin, you again would use a coppice management system. Tannin is used in the making of ink and leather. In the latter case, animal hides are softened in a pit of lime, the hair and flesh is then removed. Then, the hides are passed through tannin baths for treating, the tannin coagulating the proteins in the hide, turning it into leather. The baths are simply vats containing pounded up oak bark and water. Afterwards the leather is rinsed and dried. The tannin industry in Britain reached its peak between 1810-15 when it was using approximately 90,000 tons of bark a year. Rhayader had a thriving leather industry supporting three factories, the last closing in the 1950s.

its larva can live for two years in a wet rot hole before emerging as an adult beetle clothed in its tough armour. Holes which are damp rather than wet are attractive residences for woodlice (e.g. *Oniscus*) and woodland species of snail (e.g. *Helix*).

Dry rot holes are a valuable habitat for many terrestrial, or ground dwelling, arthropods such as centipedes and spiders who may live there throughout their lives. Others such as ladybirds (*Coccinellidae*) and bees use holes as a warm and sheltered winter refuges. Birds too make good use of these holes and some twenty species nest in them, the larger holes being used by the bigger species like the tawny owl (*Strix aluco*) and the smaller by acrobatic tits (*Parus*) or the pied fly-catcher (*Ficedula hypoleuca*). Mammals too use these holes, either as temporary shelter from weather or enemies or as more permanent homes. Bats may roost in holes in the summer months, and even in winter if the hole gives enough shelter. Squirrels too use holes for rearing their young or bedding down. Like the bats, these creatures prefer holes higher up the tree, whilst small mammals such as woodmice use those nearer the ground.

As you can imagine, rot holes are more plentiful in older trees. Unfortunately, it is not just at Gilfach that old trees, with numerous holes, are a scarce commodity. All over Britain, forestry activities and the loss of woodland to urbanization and agriculture has caused a serious reduction in the provision of such holes — with the resultant decrease in the population of many of our woodland birds and mammals, let alone specialized insects, fungi and plants. Natural disasters have also taken their toll, like the Dutch Elm Disease which ravaged the British countryside in the 1970s and the hurricanes and severe gales of 1987. So as to attract those birds and mammals that need such holes in order to rear their young, nest boxes are provided extensively as part of conservation schemes throughout the country. These boxes are designed to attract different species, from those commonly seen for sale in garden centres, which make ideal homes for birds such as the tit and pied flycatcher, but are not much good for owls, nor are they particularly attractive to the robin (*Erithacus rubecula*). The robin's designer residence is an open-fronted box, whilst the tawny owl likes a chimney-shaped structure, resembling deep dry rot holes. As you walk around Gilfach woods you will see a proliferation of nest boxes designed for specific species such as the pied flycatcher, goldcrest and tawny owl. Around the country you will see a variety of structures, some high on poles for kestrels (*Falco tinnunculus*), some on floats on lakes and gravel pits to attract various waterbirds, in farm buildings for barn owls

(*Tyto alba*), as well as boxes for bats and other mammals located in appropriate places. If you want to know more about boxes for your own garden it is worth contacting your local bat group and the British Trust for Ornithology.

Rot holes are not permanent habitats, though they may well be around for several centuries. But, sooner or later, the tree dies, and the dead wood becomes a home to a specialized and extremely important group of creatures. Known as 'detritivores' (eaters of detritus), these creatures help in the decomposition of organic matter, whether it be dead leaves, trees, animals or even animal droppings. The decomposition means that these organic tissues are broken down into carbon dioxide, water and minerals to be returned to the earth, and from there to be taken up by the plants and put back into the woodland ecosystem. Dead wood is perhaps the most important matter to be returned to the ecosystem as so much in the way of energy and nutrients are trapped in trees when they are alive. If you like, the trees are the woodland ecosystem's main bank account, releasing the money only on the death of the tree. Of course when trees are killed and removed from the woodland as timber, or dead trees cleared away, this energy bank is not given back to the woodland, which becomes progressively more impoverished. Dead wood is home to about 1,000 different animal and several hundred fungi species. It is estimated that a tidy forest, where dead wood is a rare sight, may be impoverished by up to a fifth of its potential animal life. So there are good reasons to leave fallen trees around the woods, it is not just that nature wardens are lazy!

This process of recycling nutrients and energy is crucial to the overall health of the wood – that is the trees, plants, birds, beasts, insects and fungi. On another level, if it wasn't for the decomposers, we would be wading about in deep layers of dead leaves and dead animals. Obviously some matter, such as leaves and animal droppings, are recycled quite quickly in a matter of days or weeks. Animal bones take a little longer and a large log may take twenty years to decay completely, the nutrients released and the wood disintegrated. The rate of decay depends on several factors: whether the wood was already beginning to decay whilst still alive, whether it fell somewhere where it remained moist or was it baked hard and dry by the sun, or was it burnt either by lightning, spontaneous combustion or the fires of human origin. Decomposition is slower in dry and burnt wood.

The process of decomposition can be thought of as occurring in three stages, which may occur partially in parallel. First is the breakdown of the dead material into large particles. Second, is the breakdown of these large particles into succes-

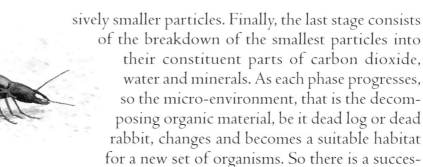

DEVIL'S COACH HORSE.

sively smaller particles. Finally, the last stage consists of the breakdown of the smallest particles into their constituent parts of carbon dioxide, water and minerals. As each phase progresses, so the micro-environment, that is the decomposing organic material, be it dead log or dead rabbit, changes and becomes a suitable habitat for a new set of organisms. So there is a succession of colonization of different decomposer species.

In the case of wood, first are the highly specialized groups which make their living from the dying or newly dead tree. At this stage the wood still contains a plentiful supply of nutrients and so the decomposers tend to be quite large. Bracket fungi and cap fungi are common during the early years of decay, sapping the nutrients from the dead wood and in turn providing food to many insects and their larvae, as well as some beetles such as the black, aptly named, devil's coach horse (*Staphylinus olens*). A variety of bark beetles are also amongst these early colonists, boring tunnels in which to lay their eggs, the larvae later burrowing out to the surface. All this tunnelling loosens the bark, enabling other creatures to enter, such as woodlice and centipedes. Deeper in the wood grow the larvae of larger beetles, including the stag beetle (*Lucanus cervus*). These infants take several years to grow, inhabiting rotten wood, before finally emerging, armoured with huge antler-like mandibles, which the beetles use mainly for wrestling matches between each other. As the wood becomes more decayed and crumbly so micro-organisms, such as multitudinous bacteria, get to work until finally there is nothing left at all.

Every autumn billions of dead leaves fall to the ground, to be broken down and returned to the soil. In much of Britain a major instigator in this process is the humble earthworm (*Lumbricus*). The earthworms pull leaves into their damp burrows where they munch away, breaking down the leaves during digestion and passing much in their excreta — those nutrient-rich little mounds we see on the lawn, earthworm casts. These in turn are quickly colonized by bacteria which continue the process of helping fertilize the soil. However, in the uplands where the soil is acidic, worms are few in number and leaves remain on the surface where they take longer to decay. This leaf litter is home to many tiny creatures who enjoy the safe cover and steady conditions of temperature and humidity provided. The layer of

STAG BEETLE.

leaf litter gradates downwards from whole leaves to those in various states of decay to the soil beneath. Though many bacteria and fungi live off the decaying matter in the lower strata, it is on the surface layer that the larger creatures are found, those we can see with the naked eye. This layer is seething with spiders and a myriad of mites, abounding with springtails (*Collembola*) and beetles. Many of these creatures are herbivores, feeding off the leaf litter and, in turn, providing food for the many carnivores around. Carnivores such as the wolf spiders (*Lycosidae*) which, if you stand quietly on a warm day, you may hear as they scuttle across the leaves in pursuit of their prey. More familiar inhabitants of the leaf litter are wood-lice which feed on leaves, seedlings, fungi and animal dung. These somewhat cumbersome creatures, also known as God's hogs, are unable to absorb all the nutri-

SPECIAL FEATURES FOR SPECIAL LIVES

In an habitat, such as an oakwood, each species of animal, plant and bird occupies an exclusive aspect of the environment. These aspects are known collectively as the species' niche and are associated with the needs of the organism to find food and to reproduce. To illustrate the different ways organisms have evolved with regard to their particular niches, I have chosen three species of bird found in Gilfach's oakwood: the tawny owl, the woodpecker and the pied flycatcher.

The tawny owl is a cat on wings, a silent, efficient bird of prey which eats small mammals, birds, fish, frogs and insects. It is most active at night when it hunts its prey and communicates with its own kind. There are good reasons for being nocturnal. For a start your prey is often out and about under the cover of darkness and you can employ the same cover to help you catch your dinner unawares. The tawny owl's familiar hoot is made up of the call of two separate birds, one going 'hooo' and the other 'kee-wick', so if you hear a 'tu-whit tu-whoo' you know you are listening to a night time conversation between two tawny owls.

The tawny roosts during the day, often being mobbed by a flock of small birds trying to move it on. The eyes are very large and this allows in more light giving better night vision. In fact their night vision is excellent, they can see in conditions where the light is 100 times poorer than we humans need. Imagine a moonless, cloudy night. As we stumble in the darkness, the owl is easily able to spot a mouse 2 metres (6.5 feet) away. The eye is very large; however, it has no mobility. The owl cannot move its eyes to look about it and compensates for this by being able to rotate its head almost in a complete circle, and thus be able to see all around it.

Even without its eyes, the owl is still an expert at getting around. Just using hearing alone, in total darkness an owl can home in on a prey item with a flight path which is accurate to within one degree. In comparison to other birds, owls have large ears (though these are not easily visible to us). The ears are situated just behind the face and are placed rather lopsidedly on the head. This asymmetry allows for greater accuracy in locating prey. For example, when the prey is directly in front of (or behind) the bird, the fractional time lag of a sound reaching the second ear, caused by the lopsided placements on the head, pinpoints, to a fine degree, the direction of the source, be it moth or mouse. Owls hear very high pitched noises, made by the high squeaky voices of rodents, and the rustling of insects and others as they move silently (at least as far as we are concerned) through the undergrowth and leaf litter.

The owl's prey also has very sharp hearing. It needs to. Its very survival depends on it being aware of any predator bearing down on it. In order to increase its stealth, the owl has adapted its wings such that flight is almost silent. The wing's leading edge has a comb-like fringe to it which breaks up the air and stops it whistling as it passes over the surface. For the same purpose of deadening the wind sound, the wing feathers have a velvety feel to them.

The woodpecker's diet is mostly of insects, especially those living on and under the bark of the tree. It also eats nuts, acorns and nestlings of other birds. It is famous for its excavation, hole-boring activities. It makes nest holes

ents they need from their food the first time it passes through the gut. So in order to get sufficient from their low quality diet, they eat their own faeces, extracting from it more of the goodness as it passes through the gut a second time. This is an adaptive behaviour they share with rabbits and for the same purpose as the cud chewing we see in sheep and cows.

Also foraging through the leaf litter is the tiny, silent, bright-eyed woodmouse. Though this is one of Britain's commonest mammals, you will be lucky indeed to see it as it gathers its daily fare of seeds and fruits. It is out and about mainly at night, spending the daylight hours in burrows, huddled together in the winter to keep warm. The woodmouse has many enemies in the wood, being prey to owls and members of the weasel (*Mustela*) family, including the rare polecat (*Mustela putorius*).

for its young, and often these are used by other species in later years. It also has been known to bore holes in artificial nest boxes used by other species and prey on the nestlings within. However, it is basically a predator of insects living on trees and thus, the major adaptations of the woodpecker revolve around how it moves and forages on this sheer, vertical surface - the tree trunk.

The first problem is climbing up and hanging on to the trunk as the woodpeckers work their way from the bottom of the trunk upwards. The woodpecker has evolved tail feathers which are rigid and stiff, and very strong. This means the tail acts as a third leg, supporting the weight of the bird. The woodpecker also has an unusual arrangement of its toes. Most bird species have three toes pointing forward and only one pointing backwards on each foot, with which to grip on to the round surface of a branch. The woodpecker has two toes pointing backwards and two pointing forwards. This again acts as a stabilizer as it moves up and down the tree.

Perhaps the obvious question regarding woodpeckers is, why don't they get headaches? Because of another adaptive feature. There is a natural shock absorber, made of cartilaginous material, located between the beak and the skull, which acts to cushion and protect the bird's brain. In order to get the insects out from under the bark the woodpecker has a special beak and tongue. The beak is short and stout with a sharp, squared-off end like a chisel. Indeed, that is how the bird works, as if it were using a hammer and chisel. Woodpeckers also have enormously long tongues, so long that when not in use, the tongue is curled up in the top of the skull! The tip of the tongue is barbed and acts to harpoon insects hiding deep beneath the bark.

The pied flycatcher is also insectivorous. However, unlike the tawny owl and woodpecker, the flycatcher does not spend all the year in Britain but is a summer visitor, spending the winter months in tropical West Africa. Its long migration means that it has to be able to eat on the wing. Like those summer aerial acrobats of open places, the swallows and swifts, the flycatcher is able to snatch insects from the air. However, the flycatcher hunts in woods and it can also take insects from the leaf of a tree as it passes. It tends to make short flights, darting from one tree to another. Because it hunts on the wing, it does not do so well in woods with a thick shrub layer. Rather, it prefers the open woodland structure, typical of grazed sessile oakwoods such as we see at Gilfach.

While all these birds are at risk from a variety of pressures, not least a loss of habitat, the pied flycatcher has an extra burden. There is a physical toll in the long flight to and from Africa every year and some birds die of exhaustion. Others are lost through being shot as they pass over countries such as Spain and Portugal where they are considered a delicacy when fried. There are International Bird Conventions which set up to protect birds and certainly this has helped reduce the destruction of small migratory birds, though it is still a cause for concern.

FOX, LISTENING FOR DINNER MOVING IN THE GRASS

The polecat population of Britain suffered a serious decline with the establishment of sporting estates across Britain. It was regarded as a wanton killer of game birds and was ruthlessly killed in turn by gamekeepers using ghastly contraptions such as the gin trap. Central Wales acted as a refuge as there was little in the way of such organized killing, though the polecat was often caught in the many traps set for the commercial hunting of rabbits. Since the first World War there has been a decline in the activities of gamekeepers, and commercial rabbit hunting became uneconomic after the devastation of myxomatosis in the 1950s combined with the legal banning of the gin trap. All of this has meant that the polecat population has made a recovery in a small number of locations in the last thirty years, though, as with most of our wildlife, it is threatened by habitat loss, such as the removal of woods and hedgerows where it hides and hunts.

The polecat is a nocturnal hunter, stalking its prey and killing them with a single bite to the neck. A large portion of its diet comprises other animals who are out and about at night: rabbits, hedgehogs, shrews, moles, voles and mice. It is also sneaky enough to take sleeping birds from their perches in hedges and trees.

The polecat is total carnivore, a species at the centre of the woodland food web. It is completely dependant on the success of the lives of the other species in the wood, the eaters and eaten; the detritivores providing nutrition for the plants which in turn are providers for insects, birds and mammals; some of whom also eat the insects, and some of whom end up as a polecat's pudding.

The polecat has few enemies, other than man (and cars) as it is well protected by

WOOD WARBLER.

its strong, offensive body odour and a sharp set of teeth. However, it may be killed by foxes who roam over Gilfach at night, hunting in the woods, along the hedges, in the fields and on the moorland. These foxes do not have the easy pickings from dustbins and kindly humans as do their city cousins. Unlike the polecat, the fox is an omnivore, like us it can eat almost anything. Whilst it certainly takes the same sort of prey as the polecat, it will also eat beetles, fruit, and in winter a major food source is found on the moorland in the form of sheep carcasses, though the odd sickly lamb may also disappear in spring. The fox has a bad reputation with farmers, even though research suggests that very few lambs are taken by them. In the wood, the fox is not a threat to the shepherd but is another constant enemy of the small mammals and birds who warily eke out their lives in the leaf litter.

In general, the woodland ecosystem is based on a four-tiered structure rising from ground level to a height of some 30 metres (98 feet). At the ground level are the smallest plants, carpets of green mosses patterned with multi-coloured fungi. Also present are many species of animals and bacteria which are responsible for the decomposition of any dead matter in the wood. This latter group will benefit from the death of those trees at Gilfach which are sacrificed to form light chimneys.

At the second level is the herb, or field layer, rising to a height of about 0.5 metres (1.6 feet), the home of woodmice. It is here that we find those wonders of the woodland, the bluebell (*Hyacinthoides non-scripta*), wood anemone (*Anemone nemorosa*) and primrose (*Primula vulgaris*). The herb layer will also benefit from the creation of glades and light chimneys at Gilfach.

The third tier or storey in the wood is the shrub or understorey layer. As its name implies, it consists of shrubs, young tree saplings and the lower branches of mature trees, up to a height of about 5 metres (16 feet). Bramble (*Rubus fruticosus*), with its dark, sweet blackberries, young holly and oak all contribute to this layer. At Gilfach this layer is not particularly prominent as little vegetation had much chance to grow this high because of the grazing sheep. However, over the next few decades, with the exclusion of grazing, this layer will soon develop and provide a nesting and feeding area for many small birds, mammals and insects.

Finally, above all, basking in the direct sunlight and sheltering those below from the rain, is the tree or canopy layer. This consists of the upper branches of the mature trees and their associated flora and fauna. Exposed to most light, this is a very green and leafy environment. As with all the layers of the wood, the canopy contains its own cycles of life within the greater cycle of the whole wood.

The young leaves provide a favoured, nutritious food for a host of insects at various stages of their lifecycles. In turn, these are eaten by brown long-eared bats and a variety of bird species such as the great and lesser spotted woodpeckers (*Dendrocopos major and Dendrocopos minor*) and common treecreepers (*Certhia familiaris*). Other birds, including buzzards, use the upper storey of the wood as sites for their large twig nests, though they hunt over open moorland. Many inhabitants of the wood are constrained to live in only one or two of the layers. Others, for instance the squirrel, use all of the layers in which to forage, feed and breed. The dainty wood warbler (*Phyllscopus sibilatrix*) with its yellow-green head and distinctive eyestripe is another such species.

The wood warbler is only in Britain during the summer, between April and August, spending the winter in the warmth of the North African forests. During its sojourn in Britain it is severely restricted to a clearly defined habitat, namely mature woodland with a close knit canopy shading the ground below producing a sparsely covered ground and herb layer. The bird feeds off insects which thrive in such woodlands. The wood warbler can be seen hovering as it deftly picks insects and caterpillars from the undersides of leaves. It is strictly a bird of the trees, only venturing from the wood to migrate. Yet oddly enough, it nests on the ground, rather than perhaps more safely in the tree itself. The female builds a dome shaped nest in a shallow hollow on the ground, the dome roof just protruding above ground level. No doubt the eggs and nestlings can make a welcome addition to the diet of a passing polecat, fox or hedgehog.

In summary then, the oakwood is a specific type of community whose structure of different layers provides a multitude of distinctive niches, or homes, for all sorts of creatures and plants. The centre of this thriving community is, of course, the oak tree itself. The wood can be considered a self-sufficient community, a closed system, requiring little from the world beyond. As with any such community, its members have specific roles to play. In human terms such roles would include farmers, builders, manufacturers, cooks, teachers, and so on. In the oakwood, the system relies on the activities of those organisms involved in the 'green plant industry', the 'soil industry' and a bit of outside help from the atmosphere and the underlying rocks. The driving force behind all this cycle of activity – birth, life, death and decomposition – is the sun. Without the energy provided by the sun, captured by the leaves and green plants, none of what we see at Gilfach, or indeed anywhere else, would exist, including ourselves.

4

TIMBER!

Like disciplined Roman legionnaires, the serried ranks of the plantations march across our upland slopes. Sombre, regimented, silent, casting an air of foreboding, these conifer woods seem to be the antithesis of the light, disorderly oakwoods which reverberate with bird song and squirrel chatter.

At Gilfach the oakwood is not the only product of the First World War. Indirectly, so is the conifer plantation which darkly covers the south-west corner of the reserve on Gamallt Hill. The Great War of 1914-19 was a watershed in British life and resulted in many cultural and economic changes. Some of these directly affected the structure of the countryside and the wildlife inhabiting it.

Since the Neolithic era, perhaps the most far reaching change in land use came in 1919 with the inauguration of the Forestry Commission. The Forestry Commission is a statutory body set up to ensure that Britain could be self-sufficient in timber. In order to fulfil this task, the commission was given powers to purchase land on which to plant its armies of conifer trees. The single-minded purpose of providing the country with a fast-growing timber source did not take account of the impoverishment such massed, angular ranks of conifers would bring to both native wildlife and human aesthetics. This attitude began to change when, with the 1968 Countryside Act, the Commission's remit expanded and it was obliged to open up its lands to tourism and recreation. More recently, there has been a shift in policy away from pure conifer stands to increasingly mixed plantations which include a variety of broadleaved, native species.

However, well before these changes, in 1959, the invading army entered Gilfach. The Forestry Commission acquired 33.6 acres (13.6 hectares) on the northern slope of Gamallt Hill and proceeded to plant a typical, if rather small, block plantation. The triangular-shaped plantation rises from 250 to 350 metres (820-1,150 feet) above sea level and comprises four distinct blocks of tree species. The largest block is 14.8 acres (6 hectares) of Dunkeld larch (*Larix x eurolepis*), a natural hybrid. Alongside lie 8.6 acres (3.5 hectares) of lodgepole pine (*Pinus contorta*), 7.4 acres (3 hectares) of Scot's pine (*Pinus sylvestris*) and 2.5 acres (one hectare) of sitka spruce (*Picea sitchensis*). The remaining area of the plantation is made up of patches of native vegetation, namely bilberry (*Vaccinium myrtillus*), ling heather (*Calluna vulgaris*) and gorse (*Ulex europaeus*).

Previous page: GAMALLT, CLAD IN CONIFER GREEN.

GAMALLT – SOMBRE GLOOM OF THE CONIFER PLANTATION.

Perhaps the most striking features of this and other conifer plantations are their darkness and quietness. The trees are planted in rows to enable easy access when planting and when the timber is harvested. They are also planted close together which provides a larger crop and helps force the trees to go straight up rather than branching, thereby keeping knots in the timber as few and as small as possible. Such close planting means that little light, or rainfall, is able to penetrate through the thick, interlacing canopy of boughs and leaves, giving the wood its murky, forbidding atmosphere. This shortage of essential light and water is one reason why there is little in the way of vegetation within the ground, herb and shrub layers.

Another factor is the increase in the acidity of the soil caused by the fall of needles from the trees. These needles have tough outer layers and are slow to decompose. Unlike leaves of broadleaved trees, pine needles contain a lot of resinous substances and little calcium. It is the release of calcium during decomposition that helps neutralize the soil within broadleaved woods, but this does not happen in the conifer plantation. So, whilst putting little back in, these rapidly growing forestry species continue to take up precious nutrients from the soil. These nutrients are then removed from the site in the form of harvested timber. Thus, there is an overall impoverishment of the soil and an increase in its acidity.

The conifers are an extremely ancient and successful group of trees. Fossil records tell us that they were growing 300 million years ago! The majority of the species do best in cool conditions and are found all over the world in areas of high latitude and/or high altitude. The group is characterized by its production of seed bearing cones, used widely in Christmas decorations. The cones are the fruiting bodies of the tree and serve a similar function – protecting the seeds until they ripen and providing a means of dispersal. Apples, for instance, are eaten by many animals and the seeds pass through the creature's gut to be deposited elsewhere, hopefully in a place suitable for germination. The principle still works even if, like me, you throw the core away rather than eat the seeds! When the conifer seeds are ripe the cone opens out exposing the seeds for dispersal by the wind or by seed eating creatures like squirrels and siskins (*Carduelis spinus*).

In the commercial world of timber, conifers are known as 'softwoods'; though this is in general a true description, it can be a somewhat misleading term as the softest woods are in fact obtained from broadleaved trees, for example balsa (*Ochroma lagopus*) and some conifers, such as the yew (*Taxaceae*), produce wood

COAL TITS – ARBOREAL ACROBATS.

which is regarded as hard! Rather the term refers to the more simple structure of this ancient tree group. Conifers do not show the variety or complexity of cell and structure organization as do the hardwoods. This means that the timber produced is less varied and more predictable. This predictability, combined with the rapid growth, means conifers are extremely important commercially.

Conifers in the main are evergreen, the major exception being the larches. Evergreens do not lose their leaves in one fell swoop as do deciduous trees. There is not the impressive autumnal change of colour and loss of leaves, as we see in Gilfach's oakwood, a mere splash being provided by the larch. The conifers shed their needle-shaped leaves throughout the year, constantly replacing the old ones

SCOTS PINE
CONE.

with new growth. If you like, this is similar to how our own hair works. Dead hair is superseded by new growth, the only 'autumnal' loss is due to age. The fact that the conifers are evergreen means that they grow throughout the year. Their growth rate is faster in spring and summer, when there is more sunlight. Sunlight is trapped by leaves and used to make the sugars necessary for growth. The densely packed leaves of conifers are extremely efficient at catching sunlight even in the short days of winter.

The conifers' rapid growth means they give a quick return on the capital investment of planting and management. The wood is used widely, some species being more appropriate for certain applications. Of the four species present at Gamallt, the Scot's and lodgepole pines are perhaps the most important. These trees contain a lot of resin which helps to preserve the wood naturally. When coated in creosote the timbers are long lasting and are used as telegraph poles and railway sleepers. The timber obtained from the Scot's pine is known as 'yellow deal', its colour resulting from the resins. This wood is often used ornamentally as in the making of furniture. Further, the living tree can be tapped for its resin which is used in the manufacture of both turpentine and of 'rosin'. The latter is used to coat the strings of instruments, such as cellos. The resins are also used in the production of paints, pharmaceutical products and even perfume.

The conical-shaped sitka spruce is a relative of the Norway spruce (*Picea abies*), the latter known to us all as the Christmas tree. The sitka spruce accounts for some 10% of the total productive softwood forest in the United Kingdom. Its wood is odourless and easy to work making it a favourite for general carpentry use and in the fashioning of stringed instruments, such as violins. It is also extensively used in the manufacture of pulp for paper, cardboard and even textiles.

The larch family is one of the smallest, containing 12 species, the Dunkeld present at Gamallt being a natural hybrid. The larches are unusual conifers in that they are truly deciduous, standing strikingly bare in the winter against the dark greens of their fellow conifers on Gamallt Hill. These pyramidal trees do not like low-lying areas which accumulate water but do well on the free-draining slopes here at Gilfach. The wood produced is strong and durable, as evidenced by its use for pit props and in the building of barges, once important for the movement of goods, now more usually associated with the movement of holiday-makers around the canals of England. The bark contains appreciable quantities of tannin which, as we saw before, is used in the treating of leather and manufacture of dyes. The tree also has medicinal properties and larch or Venice turpentine, obtained by tapping, is used by veterinary surgeons in the treatment of large animals — horses, cattle and sheep. In the summer months the leaves exude a whiteish substance known as 'larch manna' which also has medicinal properties.

Trees on plantations grow closer together than they would naturally and there is a consequent paucity of plant and animal life. The native conifer forests of Canada, for instance, contain a wide variety of birds, mammals, plants and insects. But in Britain's plantations the associated flora and fauna of these imported trees are missing. This does not mean that there is nothing living at Gamallt, for some flora and fauna do well in conifer woods and some are specialized for this habitat. However, compared to the native oakwood, the Gamallt plantation is almost deserted.

It is this scarcity and lack of variety of fauna, and in particular of song birds, which accounts for the quietness of the plantation. There is little variety of plant life so there are fewer niches for seed-eating birds, insects and insect-eating birds. Those song birds that do live in the plantation tend to be less dense in numbers

LARCH (LEFT) AND SITKA SPRUCE CONES.

GOLDCRESTS.

GOSHAWK CHASING MISTLE THRUSH.

than their counterparts in the oakwood. As a consequence there is less song, even more noticeable in the winter when the birds are no longer singing to attract mates or defend territories.

If you have sharp eyes you may notice small birds, like circus acrobats, feeding from the pine cones. These are the siskins, members of the finch family jauntily sporting yellow flecked plumage. They have short, stout bills which are tapered at the end, perfectly designed for extracting seeds from small cones. Because such seeds are not always available, the siskin will make use of other areas of the reserve in its unceasing quest for food. It tends to feed from spruce and pine trees in the spring, moving onto birch, such as those down nearer the river, in the summer and then onto alder in the winter, where it competes with its cousin, the redpoll (*Carduelis flammea*).

The earliest British reference to the siskin was in 1369, in a work of that master of storytelling, Chaucer. Over the centuries, with the deforestation of the countryside, the siskin became confined to areas of Scotland, reaching its lowest population in the 17th century. It was in the mid-1600s that it was realized that there was a timber shortage, a situation pointed out to government by the Royal Navy. Planting began in earnest and in the following century every self-respecting landowner had plantations, both of conifers and broadleaved species. Gigantic plantations sprang up, such as in Hafod, Cardiganshire, where 5 million trees were planted between 1785 and 1815. For the siskin, this was of course good news and its population began to increase. With the advent of the Forestry Commission and the timber trade's greater reliance on conifers, the bird has spread widely and in 1972 it was estimated that some 60,000 birds were resident in Britain.

Conifer bark is home to many insects. Some of these are bark beetles which, like their relatives in the oakwood, lay their eggs in the bark and the resultant larvae feed on the tree's living tissues beneath. An infestation of such pests can be a forester's nightmare as these beetle larvae can actually ring-bark the tree and kill it. But the forester has allies present, notably in the form of goldcrests (*Regulus regulus*) and coal-tits (*Parus ater*). The tiny goldcrest, Britain's smallest bird, hunts seemingly non-stop for tiny insects, spiders and their eggs. It may pass you with a somewhat distracted air. The coal-tit on the other hand is more difficult to see as it forages high up in the tree canopy. In the winter you may be more lucky as it comes down to collect and hide seeds to be relished at a later date. These tiny active birds need to work hard at maintaining their energy levels and require a lot of food. It has been estimated that a tit in winter needs the equivalent of 24 average-sized insects every minute of the day just to stay alive. Even though the coal-tits store some food this only represents a small proportion of their diet. In mid-winter coal-tits have to spend 90% of a nine hour day searching for food and, for the smaller goldcrests, this figure is probably nearer 100% and a very cold snap can severely deplete the population of these birds.

The trees at Gamallt are also home to two birds of prey, the goshawk (*Accipiter gentilis*) and its smaller relative the sparrowhawk (*Accipiter nisus*). The sparrowhawk is only 30-45 centimetres (12-18 inches) tall and is an agile hunter. It feeds off small song birds, those already mentioned along with robins and chaffinches (*Fringilla coelebs*), present both in Gamallt and in other areas of Gilfach. It catches these by skimming close to the ground, or along hedgerows, making full use of the cover to surprise its prey. This nimble predator is also responsible for the demise of larger species such as magpies (*Pica pica*), jackdaws (*Corvus monedula*) and jays, which no doubt is of some compensation to the small bird population.

Apart from man, the sparrowhawk has few enemies. One, however, is the goshawk. This bird is almost twice as big as the sparrowhawk and, though it feeds on similar foods, it will take much larger prey including its smaller cousin. Both birds are known to nest at Gamallt but really this dense coniferous wood is the preserve of the more agile sparrowhawk, the goshawk preferring more mature, open woodland.

The rank formation in which the trees are planted down the hillside has the effect of creating direct routes for rainfall to run off down to the Marteg at the foot of the hill. Before reaching the Marteg, however, the water has to traverse the old railway track, dropping over rocky outcrops, created by the railway builders. These are covered in a mantle of moss and fern species – a veritable fairy grotto, overhung by silver birch. Like lichens, mosses are primitive plants having no true leaves, stems or roots, but absorbing water and nutrients over their entire surface. They are most noticeable in the winter landscape, decorating the trees, ground and rocks with bright green. Many species grow during the winter and are most luxuriant in early spring after the winter growth. In the spring they produce their spore capsules, tiny time bombs waiting to explode and release the precious spores, or seeds, to the wind for dispersal and continuation of the next generation. As the summer progresses the mosses dry and wither, beginning the cycle once more in the damp autumnal weather.

The area around the railway track is more open to both sunlight and rainfall. In ditches alongside, and in puddles of water on the old track, grow ivy-leaved water crowfoot (*Ranunculus hederaceus*) studding the water surface with their white star-shaped flowers. The bed of the track comprises stony and disturbed ground and on it grow plants typical of such places. Here is the pink flowered, broad-leaved willowherb (*Epilobium montanum*) and wavy bittercress (*Cardamine flexuosa*) whose white flowers adorn the zig-zagging stem. The leaves of this latter plant are edible and resemble watercress in flavour.

These wetter conditions alongside the track and downslope towards the river provide a suitable habitat for a few species of fungi. These detritivores make full use of the annual leaf fall of the birch and larch in this area. Here on an autumnal walk you may find the butter cap (*Collycia butyracea*), so named because of its greasy feel. Here too is the penny bun fungus (*Boletus edulus*).

Over the next few years Gamallt will alter radically. To increase its wildlife potential, the Radnorshire Wildlife Trust intends to open up glades and plant broadleaved trees: sessile oak, birch, rowan and hawthorn. Some of these will be intermingled with conifers already present, providing a mixed woodland habitat. Other areas will be purely broadleaved trees, whilst some pure conifer habitat will be kept for specialist species, like the siskin and goldcrest. The greater variety of tree species will benefit these birds by giving them wider foraging opportunities, especially during the winter months. Nest boxes of an assortment of shapes and sizes will be provided

SPARROWHAWK PURSUING FINCH.

both for the species currently present and to attract others. Any conifer saplings encroaching on the sensitive areas around the fairy grottoes, river bank and hillside flushes will be unceremoniously removed! These alterations are designed to make the best use of the land both for the wildlife and for the visitors. As with all land management, the maintenance of the new-style Gamallt will be a never-ending job of vigilance.

LIFE IN THE FAST LANE

As you stand in Gilfach, surrounded by hills, looking down the valley, you will most likely feel the movement of the air around you – still days are uncommon in this part of the world. But the wind brushing your cheeks, or supporting you as you lean into the hill, is not the only thing here with the power of movement. The River Marteg, bubbling in places, boiling in others, is continually dynamic, forever moving. This perpetual motion means that the river is an extremely intricate habitat providing a thin ribbon of life which is unpredictable.

From its source, north-east of St Harmon, to where it joins the waters of the River Wye at Gilfach, the Marteg is only some 6.2 miles (10 kilometeres) long. It is a typical Welsh upland stream, but of course, little in life is ever typical. For convenience we can liken rivers to the stages of the life of man. Upland rivers with their fast flowing waters, waterfalls and whirlpools can be considered 'young'. Later, as they enter the wide valleys of the lowlands, they are termed 'mature'. At last, as they near the sea and meander, looping their way in a seemingly aimless manner, they reach 'old age'. This analogy is a useful way of visualizing a river as it travels from its source to the sea, but it is only partially true. Many rivers do not conform. A good example lies just west of Gilfach, the River Elan. The Elan is an upland river, which also meets the Wye near Rhayader. Yet up on the hills of the now flooded Elan Valley, alongside the old Aberystwyth road, it performs a delightful series of meanders along a gentle broad valley. By no means can this river be considered mature! The river's flow and appearance is dependent on the rocks beneath it, the slope of the land and the amount of rain or melted snow that feeds it. In turn these characteristics determine the life that can live in and alongside it.

Let me take you back a few thousand years to the first chapter of this book and the retreat of the ice from this part of Wales. On its retreat the ice left substantial amounts of debris, millions of tons of it, in the valley and on the slopes. This debris has, over time, washed to the valley floor and has been, and is being, cut into and washed away by the incessant movement of the waters of the River Marteg. At the same time, released from their incalculable burden of ice, the rocks beneath have risen, as when pressure is removed from a coiled spring. Wales is still rising and the river is still cutting. Imagine we could cut a profile, a cross-section, across Gilfach valley through the river. We would see the broad U-shape of Gilfach as we see now, and we would notice a smaller V-shape at the bottom of the valley containing the River Marteg.

PREVIOUS PAGE: THE MARTEG, A RIVER OF CALMS AND WATERFALLS.

The ice has not only affected the cross-section of the river but also its path as it flows through Gilfach to its confluence with the Wye at Marteg Bridge. During this short journey it is a river of change. Shallow flowing waters give way to rapids and the tumult of Ffrwd Fawr, commonly known as 'Ffrwd Falls' – the name is better translated as 'great torrent'. Further downstream, deep languishing pools are interspersed with rocky shallows and small, teardrop-shaped islands where the water, now more turbulent, riffles. What strikes the land-based human is the roughness of the water, its inhospitability. It is full of rocks of all sizes, pebbles to boulders lie strewn as the debris of a demolition site. As the river swiftly flows, it performs three tasks: first, it removes rainwater from the land upstream, second it transports small pebbles and rock rubble downstream and, finally, through the abrasive action of this rubble, it erodes the underlying rock. However, as some aspects of the underlying geology are hard rocks, they do not wear away so easily and remain as the boulders and falls we see sticking out of the rushing waters, like the protruding bones of the earth's skeleton.

This process of erosion is most spectacular at Ffrwd Fawr. It is hard immediately to see what is happening here, amidst the roiling waters. The rocks now forming the falls are not so easily eroded by the action of the water, though being worn away they certainly are. The falls are formed because the water is eroding the rock in an irregular manner along lines of weakness caused by geological faults. The water basically exploits these vulnerable points, wearing them away faster than the surrounding harder rocks. Over thousands of years the falls will slowly recede upstream and the local ordnance survey map will need redrawing.

At this point the river bed is not smooth but makes a series of big drops, somewhat akin to a roller coaster ride, but with the added thrill of the water eddying back on itself forming whirlpools. This is the most turbulent section of the river at Gilfach – a point worth remembering when considering the salmon (*Salmo salar*) which have to traverse this section. On the positive side, all this turbulent white water, gushing over the rocks and passing through mid-air means that the river is able to collect a lot of oxygen which benefits plants and animals further downstream.

Whilst the river profile is not a smooth, gentle downward slope but is full of dips and drops, the rocks and pebbles forming the river bed are smooth. Pick up a pebble from the stream bed and it will feel silky smooth, as if polished with care. All the surfaces within the river channel are, or eventually will be, rounded in this way. This polishing is due to the action of the water rubbing the stones together, known as mutual attrition. At Ffrwd Fawr we can see this in action quite clearly. You may notice, if the river is not in flood, small potholes in the rock surface, some of which contain a pebble or two, spinning around in the eddying water. These pebbles act like drill bits, boring into the rock, remorselessly lowering the river bed. Pebbles can also drill horizontal channels into the rock, scraping away the surface as they are pitched at speed downstream. These horizontal grooves are descriptively called 'flutes', reminiscent of elegant glassware.

Bodies of freshwater come in a variety of types – ponds, lakes, deep rivers and shallow mountain streams, such as the Marteg. Each has its own ecosystem with specialized organisms adapted for living within, beside and above it. These organisms share the need for water for all or part of their lifecycles. In each system the qualities related to this common factor vary considerably in terms of volume of water, speed of the current, chemical composition, oxygen content and temperature.

The Marteg is like a petulant child, forever changing its mood, never seeming to be pleased with the status quo. To discover the cause of all this inconsistency and unpredictability we must look to the hills. For it is the hills that feed the Marteg its diet of rain. These hills shape the river's catchment area. Mid-Wales does not enjoy a hot, sunny climate, consequently relatively little of the rain that falls evaporates. Rather, when a raindrop lands it has two possibilities open to it: either to sink into the soil and rock or to travel over the surface. Whichever route, most of the rainfall will end up in the river and only a small proportion will be used by plants and animals.

The Marteg catchment comprises hard, slatey rocks which are impermeable to water and thus the option of sinking through the rocks is unavailable. Further, the soil layer is not deep and thus has little capacity to hold water – at least on the slopes of the hills. Soil is made up of particles and is not a continuous mass but full of tiny holes. These holes trap air and water. However, the water droplets seep continually downhill, forming underground rivulets. These have recently been identified by soil scientists as 'pipes' and are characteristic of slopes in mid-Wales. One of the striking aspects of this part of Wales is the openness of the hillsides; there are few tall plants or trees. Tall plants would reduce the amount of rain reaching the soil, catching it in their leaves and trapping it amongst their roots. The lack of such interceptors, combined with the mattedness of the hillside

SALMON LEAP.

vegetation means that substantial amounts of rain quickly run over the surface down to the river. A heavy downfall can thus have a dramatic effect on the river's depth, volume and speed of flow, thereby changing the river's whole character in a matter of hours. Not only does such a spate increase these physical characteristics of the water, it also means the river is able to carry more debris downstream, increasing erosion and turbulence. This is known as a flashy response, as unpredictable as Jumping Jack Fash himself.

In contrast, in a dry summer the river can become extremely shallow, some parts of the channel floor empty of water. In such circumstances, the speed of the river's flow is slower and the water contains less oxygen and is considerably warmer.

CRYSTAL CLEAR WATERS?

Clear mountain streams such as the Marteg do not tend to remind us of pollution. Rather we consider them as fresh and pure, an image well used by the advertising profession. These are not the waters disfigured by old car tyres, prams, plastic bags and other unsightly signs of human waste. Nor the smelly, foaming waters associated with outflows from sewage or industrial works. No – the pollution affecting these rivers is far more sinister because it is invisible.

The uplands of Britain are not heavily industrialized, but are areas of farming activity. The ground is naturally acidic and this is reflected both in the acid nature of the rivers and the wildlife which is adapted to such conditions. But one can have too much of a good thing. Much of our upland landscape is covered in forestry plantations, as represented by Gamallt. These increase the acidic nature of the soil in two ways. First, conifers effectively trap airborne pollutants in their thick foliage. These pollutants then further acidify drops of rain running down the tree to the ground. Secondly, the conifer trees use up nutrients which are removed from the area in the form of commercial timber. Also the regular rows of planting increase the leaching of the soil and nutrients are only marginally replaced by the pine needles which are slow to decompose. The overall result is that the land and waters become ever more acidic, a threat to wildlife which can no longer tolerate the conditions.

Pollutants have a similar cumulative effect. The annual use of pesticides, fertilizers and sheepdips can have a lethal effect on a species either by directly killing individuals, or more subtly, by reducing their breeding potential. In the 1950s and 1960s the otter suffered a serious decline across the country, becoming extinct in some areas. Whilst this was partly due to habitat destruction, agrochemicals were certainly also to blame. These substances are washed into the waterways and absorbed by plankton. The plankton are eaten by invertebrates and they in turn by fish. At each stage of the food chain the chemicals become more concentrated in the tissues of the organism so that top predators, such as the otter, receive large doses with each fish eaten. A hearty meal of too many poisoned fish could lead to outright death. Sub–lethal effects account for the decline in population. Birds such as dippers and grey wagtails also suffered. Data from 'unspoilt' areas such as mid–Wales showed that these birds were unable to breed successfully. Whilst they laid fertile eggs, the shells tended to be thin and fragile, thus cooling more quickly or breaking – either way spelling death for the growing chick inside. Indeed, the embryo chicks themselves were less hardy, many dying in the egg. Though modern chemicals tend to be more eco–friendly, one should not assume that this means they are safe. And this is only in the uplands. Worse still are the chemical rich waters of the industrial, urbanized lowlands of Britain.

A more dramatic destruction of life through pollution occurs when there is a sudden spillage of some chemical. For example, a farmer illegally disposing of sheepdip or a spillage from a local timber processing site can cause rapid death of river life. This is indicated by the masses of dead and dying fish found below where the chemical entered the waters.

The river pattern is a slim trickle interspersed with deeper pools. Much more of the rocks at the falls are exposed, trapping small shallow pools in their indentations.

So how do the animals who live in the river cope with such an unpredictable home? In dry conditions, fish restrict their movements to the deeper areas, and insects, whose larvae live in the water, such as mosquitoes, midges and gnats, lay drought resistant eggs which do not hatch until water conditions become more favourable. Extremely dry conditions are rare in the Marteg. Rather the habitat in this mountain stream is characterized by the fast flow of water and the attendant conditions associated with such speedy water.

A fast current washes downstream any plant or creature which cannot hang on, swim strongly or shelter from the current's pull. Microscopic, free-floating organisms, the planktons, have a life purely dependent on the whim of the water. Where they go, and at what speed, is out of their control. Larger species have evolved adaptations to enable them to control their life in the fast lane. It is not an easy existence, as indicated by the fewer varieties of organisms living in mountain streams as compared to more predictable, gentler habitats such as lakes and ponds.

From what I have said so far, you may be forgiven for thinking that the river has a single current speed in any particular stretch, as, for instance, in the shallow reaches near the track running up to the farmhouse. But stand on the bridge and contemplate the river here, imagine yourself a tiny creature. Consider the weaves of the bank, the shape and size of the pebbles and the odd stick stuck in the stream bed. Look at the water, the tiny eddies, backflows, faster threads of current and slower patches near the bank. The river in miniature is full of different micro-habitats, as varied as the sections we see as we follow its total path through the valley. These micro-habitats are exploited by the river inhabitants.

Water flows freely until it meets an object; then the friction generated where the two different surfaces meet slows the current down. This means that even pebbles slow the water and immediately downstream of the pebble, the water is essentially still. This is a property shared both by water and air and integral to the design of fast cars, boats and airplanes — aptly known as streamlining. These tiny areas of quiet water are essential to the survival of many tiny creatures. The water shrimp (*Gammarus pulex*), a minute relative of those we see served as hors d'oeuvres, moves from one sheltered spot to another, avoiding being swept away by the faster currents millimetres above its head. The shrimp is beautifully designed for such a lifestyle. It somewhat resembles fast car or an upside-down boat. Its streamlined top half means that water flows over it, minimizing any drag effect. This is accentuated by the way in which the shrimp's scales are laid on its body. Tucked one under the other like roof tiles, or fish scales, their narrower side faces the creature's head, upstream. The shrimp has a distinct behaviour pattern called 'positive rheotaxis', a tendency to point its head upstream, its body cutting through the water. The shrimp's under surface is quite flat, enabling it to grasp onto the stones beneath as it works its way from one pebble to another.

The shrimp is not totally confined to the rock surfaces, as it is able to swim short distances. Others, however, are restricted in their movements to crawling about on the less turbulent surfaces of the stream bed. In particular, the nymphs, or larvae, of the mayflies (*Ephemeroptera*), stoneflies (*Plecoptera*), dragonflies and damselflies (*Odonata*). These creatures only live above the water as adults and then only for a short period of time. The dragonflies have an adult life of a few months, the stoneflies of a few weeks and the aptly named ephemeral mayflies of just a few hours or days. The earlier, nymphal, stages of the lifecycle of all these species occur beneath the surface of the water and can last for several years. The word 'nymph' refers to legendary, semi-divine maidens, suggesting sylph-like beauty. Indeed, these creatures are long and slim, some with elegant tails (mayflies having three and stoneflies two). But there, I fear the resemblance ends. Whilst the young of some species are vegetarian, browsing the algae on the stream bed, others, in particular the dragonfly nymphs, might be likened to crocodiles. They await passing prey, even as large as tadpoles, snatching them from the current with their hinged extensible jaws. Be they browsers or hunters, these nymphs are admirably suited to their watery lives. They have low-slung, flattened bodies, shaped like elongated tear-drops. With their clawed feet, they grip the pebbly surface and have a tendency to cling to surfaces. These physical and behavioural adaptations keep the nymphs in a world of relatively still water in the midst of the fast lane.

Along large sections of the bank edge the water can move at a more gentle pace. These areas are attractive homes for many species, including those already mentioned. Some are totally dependent on the quieter reaches, be they in the banks or just downstream of large boulders. These plants and animals are unable to withstand the faster currents, not being able to swim as well as say the shrimp. Rather they depend on a variety of methods to attach themselves firmly to the stream bed.

Midge larvae have suckers on their rear ends. These act as suction cups, allowing the animal to wave in the current and catch pieces of passing food. Perhaps the most interesting group of these stream bed creatures are the larvae of caddis flies. There are nearly 200 species of caddis fly (*Trichoptera*) in Britain, all of whom depend on water for the early stages of their life. Some, like the midges, have suckers, others have grappling hooks with which they attach themselves to the minute rough patches of the rock surface. Others produce a water-resistant glue to stick themselves firmly to a rock. The name 'caddis' comes from the Old English word for a 'peddlar', the man who sold almost anything and wandered the country with samples of his wares attached to his clothes. The larva spins a sticky web over its body to which it attaches grains of sand, fragments of pebble and twigs. Some species are predators and this protective coating acts as camouflage allowing the creature to lure its prey into a false sense of security. The covering also acts to protect the larva from being eaten by fish, its twiggy, rough coat jabbing into the fish's mouth. Both browser and predatory species are able to lumber about, like medieval knights in full armour, attaching themselves with their grappling hooks.

Plants living in an upland stream also have adaptations to save them being washed downstream. Like the animals, many are streamlined to reduce the drag in the passing water. Some are even coated in a slimy substance which further reduces frictional drag. Larger plants have well developed root systems, buried amongst the pebbly stream bed and securing them tightly. Such plants only grow where the river current is slow enough that it deposits some of the particles of soil and rock it is carrying. This sediment not only provides a substance for the plant to cling to but also a source of nutrients, needed as much by these plants as by a large tree. As the plant grows, its leaves and stems wave in the current and break up the water flow, creating micro-habitats for a variety of those animals we have already discussed. There are several species of water plants in the Marteg, the romantic blue of the water forget-me-not (*Myosotis scorpioides*) contrasts with the brash yellow of the lesser spearwort (*Ranunculus flammula*). If you pick the leaves of the water mint (*Mentha aquatica*) you cannot help but notice the minty smell. The slender greeny-yellow leaves of the water pepper (*Polygonum hydropiper*) contain an acid substance which makes the skin itch. Ironically, this property made the plant useful when placed deep in mattresses, because it repelled fleas, who also make the skin itch as they nibble you in the night. At the edges of the stream, where many of these plants grow, they are sometimes covered in water and sometimes not; either way, the ground beneath them is always wet if not submerged. Many grow both in the stream and on the boggy reaches of the bank.

The only plants that can truly survive on the nutrient poor, pebbly stream bed are the mosses and algae which can obtain their necessary nutrients from the rock surfaces, just like their non-aquatic relatives. Mosses cling on to the rocks by sending tiny roots, known as 'rhizoids', into the micro-cracks of the pebble surface. In the Marteg these are represented by willow moss (*Fontinalis antipyretica*), so named because of its fire-resistant properties, and *Brachythecium rivulare* which, as with many mosses, has no common name, but can be identified by its bright golden-green colour. The mosses and algae form an important part of the food chain, being eaten by herbivorous insects, snails and fish. The algae attach themselves to the rock surfaces by minute root-like structures called 'filaments'.

The water in the Marteg is rather acidic, partly because much of it arrives in the river having soaked through the upland soil and absorbed acidic ions of minerals contained in the soil. Also because of the fast flow, little organic material, such as leaves, remain in the water to be decomposed. Such a nutrient-poor stretch of water is known as 'oligotrophic'. One aspect of this is that there is little calcium available in the water. This in turn affects the number and variety of shell-bearing creatures we are likely to find in the river, creatures such as snails. As you may recall this is also true on the land, where the acidic soils also contain little calcium and snails are not prolific. The acidic nature, and speed of flow are responsible for the paucity of plant life in the river, in turn reflected in the paucity of insect life and the consequent lack of variety in the species of fish present. Once again all of this relates back to the underlying geology of the area.

The fish are the only creatures able to fully exploit the open water of the river. They are active animals which need to keep moving in order to breathe properly and to maintain body temperature, as well as to save themselves being swept downstream. In order to be able to combat the river current, fish are streamlined and, like the shrimp, show 'positive rheotaxis', that is they tend to swim upstream — a bit like running up the down escalator. Facing upstream means that the fish are orientated in the right direction to be aware of any passing food items and to benefit from the oxygen in the water.

Fish require a lot of oxygen to fuel their activity. They obtain the oxygen from water passing through their gills which are well supplied with blood vessels, in a way similar to our own breathing. The fast flow of the Marteg ensures that it contains a rich supply of oxygen. However, it only supports a few species of fish and few in number. This is because there is little food available, insects and plants are not in abundance. As a consequence fish in this river are not large like the pike (*Esox iucius*) and perch (*Perca fluviatilis*) of more nutrient-rich rivers. The species found in the Marteg include the grayling (*Thymallus thymallus*), salmon, stone-loach (*Nemacheilus barbatula*), brown trout (*Salmo fario*) and the bullhead (*Cottus gobio*), also known as the Miller's Thumb. All of these have the ability to survive in, and indeed are adapted to, the cold temperature of the Marteg waters, which ranges between 7° and 17°C. All of these species are carnivores, situated at the top of the

WETLAND WOODS

Forming leafy curtains along the banks of the Marteg are stretches of alder carr. The alder tree is a close relation of the slender birch tree. One of our few native trees, the alder can grow to a height of 20 metres (65 feet) and live for 200 years. It is restricted to damp and boggy areas alongside bodies of water. It was once a common tree, dominating the low-lying marshy areas of Britain. However, much of this sort of land has been drained, reclaimed for agriculture and building. Because it grows rapidly over the first ten years of its life, it can quickly colonize flooded areas. It makes use of the river alongside to disperse its water-resistant seeds, which are also borne on the wind or passed in the excreta of birds and animals which feed on the cone-like alder fruits.

The alder has a special adaptation which enables it to do well in nutrient-poor, leached soils. Along its roots it has tomato-sized swellings called 'nodules'. Inside these nodules live microscopic bacteria called *Frankia alni*, which can absorb precious nitrogen directly from the soil. This they turn into a form suitable for use by the tree. In return for this service the alder provides the bacteria with both protection and sugars manufactured in the leaves. A classic symbiotic relationship.

The tree also provides a home to mosses and lichens as well as many insects. Tiny yellowish bumps on the leaves are galls produced by the mite *Eriophyes laevis*. Alder-fly (*Sialis lutaria*) can be seen flitting around the branches overhanging the water, whilst the sticky, dark-green leaves are munched by a variety of moth caterpillars including the cutely named alder kitten (*Cervra bicuspis*). That rather drab member of the tit family, the marsh tit (*Parus palustris*) nests here as well as in the oakwood. Another resident is the redpoll, a small finch typical of northern areas of birch scrub. Proudly dressed in its red cap and bib, this bird depends on birch and alder seed as its main form of food. Wet alder woods, such as here at Gilfach, provide sanctuaries for otters. These bashful creatures use the gnarled and twisted exposed roots of the alder as day-time rest sites, called 'couches', before they venture forth on their nightly hunting trips.

Man too has made great use of the alder. Its leaves are attractive to fleas, and used to be scattered on the floor of homes to be swept up later and disposed of – fleas and all. Like the oak, its bark contains tannins, which are used, amongst other things, as black clothes dye. Its essence was also used to treat swellings and inflammations. The wood itself is remarkably water-resistant and was used to make water pipes and pumps as well as timbers for use in wet areas; indeed much of Venice rests on alder. Alder is not a good conductor of heat, a virtue exploited by clog makers to give a shoe that kept one's feet warm. This also means the wood burns slowly and thus, although it is not good firewood, it does make high quality charcoal, one of the best for the manufacture of gunpowder.

But the alder was not always regarded as a lucky tree and in Ireland was meant to bring misfortune to the traveller who passed by alders on a journey. For all its useful properties, felling an alder was regarded with suspicion. When freshly cut the wood is white, but exposure to the air makes it turn a reddish-orange. This was thought to indicate the bleeding of the tree's resident spirits. More pragmatic souls regarded this colouring of the wood as an aesthetic property to be fashioned into bowls, cabinets and chairs. It is not for nothing that the alder is also known as 'Scottish Mahogany'.

BULLHEAD BLENDING WITH THE STREAM FLOOR.

food chain. Each species occupies a different food niche in the stream ecosystem. Whilst they may prey on the same food types to some extent, they all have different lifestyles and means of capturing their meat.

The stone-loach and bullhead both employ guerilla tactics in order to catch unwary nymphs. To help them they both have camouflaged skin, with a pebbly pattern, enabling them to hide amongst the stones of the stream bed, the loach using much of the stream whilst the bullhead tends to lurk under bridges and areas covered by overhanging trees. The bullhead is aptly named with its large head, clownish mouth and vicious spines projecting from its head. These act as a deterrent to potential predators. Many a dead fish-loving bird has been found with a bullhead stuck in its throat. The bullhead only reaches a length of about 12 centimetres (5 inches) in an upland stream like the Marteg, yet marine variations of this species have been known to grow 2 metres (6.6 feet) in the cold waters around Greenland. The more streamlined loach gets its name from the French word '*locher*', which means to fidget, probably due to its habit, when thunderstorms approach, of rising to the surface and fidgeting noticeably. It is considered a delicacy in France, but you would need to catch a considerable number, as it is only 8-10 centimetres (3-4 inches) long!

The brown trout, or common river trout, is a browny-green, mottled fish which inhabits the deeper pools below Ffrwd Fawr. These fish have a high metabolic rate and require a lot of oxygen, more than most other species. Brown trout can grow to a hefty weight, but this is dependent on the amount of food available and large fish are not common in the Marteg. Trout are not fussy eaters and will eat almost anything, insects foolish enough to hover near the surface, nymphs, fish eggs, including those of their own species and even other fish. Voracious predators, they are the ravagers of the river.

Grayling are so named because of their greyish colour, they also go under the romantic names of 'lady of the stream' and 'flower of the water'. Whilst this may reflect their physical beauty (and delicious taste) it has little to do with their behaviour. These innocent looking fish are the sharks of the river. It is not their eating habits which get them this reputation, for they are soft mouthed feeders relying on insect larvae and other soft creatures for their diet, being particularly partial to grasshoppers unfortunate enough to land in the stream or mayflies passing over the surface. The grayling's hunting strategy is acrobatic to say the least, and its determination daunting! The fish lies on the bottom, stealthily keeping close to the stream bed, with an eye on the waters above. If a fly or some such lands on the water above and ahead of it, it will slowly move nearer, like a stalking cat. So imperceptible is the motion that the fly is caught before it is even aware of the predator approaching from below. If the prey item passes directly above, the fish goes into full acceleration, darting upwards with powerful thrusts of its large dorsal fin and tail, to grab the unsuspecting morsel. If the grayling misses, it merely tries again, being known to make forty attempts at the same piece of bait dangled by a teasing angler! The grayling is not only an efficient hunter, it is also the river bully, especially towards the brown trout who often share the same areas of river.

Salmon, whilst the largest fish in the Marteg, are the least of the predators. The adult salmon returning to the Marteg to breed after a year or more at sea, eat little or nothing during their time in the freshwaters of the rivers leading to the spawning grounds. This is rather surprising given the amount of energy these creatures use in order to bring the next generation into the world. The salmon's freshwater journey starts at the mouth of the River Wye at Chepstow, some 120 miles (190 kilometres) away. The fish swim against the current, recognizing the waters of both the Wye and the Marteg from their individual chemical composition, smell if you like. There are several obstacles in the way on their journey, not least Ffrwd Fawr, which they have to leap in order to finally reach the quieter stretches of the upper Marteg in which to spawn. The female first digs a trough in the stream bed in which to lay her precious eggs, between 10,000 and 20,000 of them, before returning down river to the sea and food. The males have just as hard a swim, culminating in fighting amongst themselves for the female's favour. This aggression causes them to lose even more condition than the females and they have less chance of surviving the return trip to the sea.

Many of the salmon eggs and newly hatched fry end up as someone's dinner, possibly that of the summer visiting goosanders (*Mergus merganser*). Those that do survive spend a couple of years growing in the Marteg before they wend their way seawards. As they grow, so their diet changes from microscopic organisms to insect larvae, the young fish feeding voraciously. On reaching a length of around 20 centimetres (8 inches), they head to the sea where food is abundant and during the following year the young salmon grow rapidly before returning as adults to commence breeding.

The river is not an isolated ecosystem, but interconnects with the land alongside. One way in which this occurs is through the food chain. Many land creatures use the river as a source of food, the river waters containing a variety of foods, albeit somewhat limited; plants, insects and fish. Some predators are piscivores, fish-eaters to you and me. The dazzling kingfisher (*Alcedo atthis*), in his royal finery, lives by the river throughout the year feeding on small fish and no doubt is responsible for the demise of many salmon fry. A small creature, the kingfisher tenderizes its catch by beating it against a branch.

A much larger bird, perhaps better known to those of us who traverse the canals, is the grey heron (*Ardea cinerea*). Standing over a metre (3 feet) tall, this is truly the assassin of the river bank. Basically a fish eater, it will readily dispatch frogs and small mammals to vary its diet. Standing crouched and motionless on the bankside it silently and patiently waits for its prey to pass by in the waters below. The heron has a long, slender neck which kinks like a coiled spring. And, like a coiled spring, the heron straightens its neck rapidly, stabbing its unwitting

SUMMER VISITORS – GOOSANDERS ABOVE GILFACH.

prey with its long sword-like beak. The heron's eyes are well placed for this mode of hunting. The heron looks down the length of its beak in the same way as a sniper would look through the sites of a rifle. Herons can have extensive hunting ranges which are long and narrow, following the course of a river for 12 miles (19 kilometres) or more, so those at Gilfach range further up and down the Marteg. As with many other river species, they are threatened by loss of feeding habitat from the diversion of waterways underground, the drainage of marshes, and the straightening of banks and removal of vegetation as well as pollution. Any loss of nest sites is exacerbated by the birds' breeding habits. The heron has a strong sense of family history, not only are individual birds loyal to nest sites, but sites may be in use for hundreds of years. These sites are usually colonies, with several birds meeting together to breed, so any loss of nest site would affect many pairs.

———

A resident fish-eater you will be fortunate indeed to see as it goes about its business is the shy, yet playful otter (*Lutra lutra*). Relying on fish for some 90% of its diet, the otter will also eat frogs and small mammals. As with many carnivores, the otter is an opportunistic eater. Though fast, he is not the fastest of Gilfach's swimmers, and prefers to hunt the slower loach and bullhead rather than tire himself out chasing grayling and trout. During the breeding season of the salmon, when many of the adult fish are nearing the end of their lives, they no doubt are a welcome addition to the otter's menu.

The same problems of habitat destruction and water pollution that affect the heron also threaten the otter. On top of this the otter was hunted for many centuries for both sport and because of its unpopularity amongst fisherman. Otters reached worryingly low numbers in the 1960s; hunting was banned in 1978, and otters, like bats, are now protected. Numbers are slowly rising, due to various factors, such as habitat protection. Gilfach is a small, yet important part of this process. The Marteg is a major waterway for these creatures whose search for food along the rivers may cause them to travel distances of 25 miles (40 kilometres) or more.

HERONS – ASSASSINS OF
THE RIVER BANK.

LARGE RED DAMSELFLIES IN MATING POSTURE.

Though the otter spends the majority of its time on land, it is highly dependent on water for the provision of its food. The otter is extremely well adapted for its life of hunting in water, even in such cold mountain streams as the Marteg. Its torpedo-shaped body cuts through the water, enhanced by the way its front feet tuck flat against its sides. An otter can swim at speeds of one metre per second, approximately 2 miles per hour. It is very agile, twisting and turning over and under the obstacles beneath the water. The power for all this is provided by the strong and flexible muscles of the back and tail. These propel the otter forwards in an undulating dolphin-like movement. Steering and additional power is provided by the webs between the toes of all four feet, which act as miniature paddles.

It is one thing to be able to move underwater, but to hunt efficiently you must also be able to detect your prey. Otters hunt both day and night. As you may have noticed, water distorts light and makes it difficult for us to see shapes clearly or judge distances. The otter has the remarkable ability of being able to change the shape of the lens of its eyes. This compensates for the light distortion, allowing the otter to see as clearly under the water as it does in the air. At night, or in murky, muddy waters this ability does not help so much. Yet the otter can still catch fish using its long, sensitive whiskers to detect changes in the water current which indicate the location of a swimming fish.

The final special adaptation of the otter is not so much to do with its ability to swim or locate prey, but with keeping warm and dry. The otter's coat is of the same basic design as that of most mammals, an outer layer of stiff, stout guard hairs and an undercoat of finer hairs. The guard hairs are slightly oiled (as are those of our cats, dogs and selves) and serves to keep water out. The fine undercoat provides a layer of insulation. It is this same design which allows many of our dog breeds to spend time playing in and out of the water without getting wet through. The only difference between their coats and those of otters is the otter's coat is longer (in proportion to its body size) and substantially denser or thicker, there being some 600 hairs per square millimetre. Whilst only a minor alteration in coat design, this adaptation means that otters can spend many hours of every day (or night) immersed in water.

If you wander quietly along the Marteg you may catch sight of one of the more

THE DIPPER, 'BESSIE DUCKER'. Opposite: OTTER ABOUT TO TAKE THE PLUNGE.

endearing residents, the dipper (*Cinclus cinclus*). Known as 'Bessie Ducker', this dainty bird is similarly shaped to the wren. Clothed in respectable brown with a bright white bib, this bird is unique in being able to walk under water in the fast currents of the Marteg. Its strong feet enable it to grip the pebbly bottom and it uses its wings as underwater propellers allowing it to swim after its prey of aquatic insects and small fish. Unlike that other underwater bird, the penguin (*Spheniscidae*), the dipper is just as agile in the air and often will be seen skimming the surface of the river after mayflies and dragonflies – a skill it shares with that other silent hunter of the river surface, Daubenton's bat. Another important insect eater is the grey wagtail (*Motacilla cinerea*), which you may recognize by his lemon yellow breast. This bird has an extra-long tail which it uses as a counterbalance when walking down the sides of the slippery stones of the river bed.

Whilst the insects hovering over the water surface are tasty meals for others, some are hunters in their own right. For as the poet Swift so neatly described a food chain:

> Nat'ralists observe a flea
> Hath smaller fleas that on him prey,
> And these have smaller still to bite 'em,
> And so proceed *ad infinitum*.

One such group of hunters is the dragonflies and damselflies. Easily confused in flight, these two groups are distinguishable when at rest, dragonflies rest with their wings outstretched whilst damselflies demurely fold them together above the body. Dragonflies are strong fliers, hawkishly patrolling a stretch of stream in pursuit of mosquitoes, mayflies, midges and gnats. These are sight predators, detecting the slightest movement with their huge compound eyes, containing some 30,000 hexagonal lenses. Like owls, they are unable to move their eyes, and thus are aided in the hunt by having long slender necks on which they rotate their heads, giving almost all round vision. The damselflies are lazier creatures, spending much of their time resting on vegetation, rousing themselves to hunt amongst the bankside verdure. Here they will find the nectar loving caddis fly, which sucks the sweet essence from the flowering plants growing along the river bank.

The river bank is a rather smudged boundary between the aquatic environment of the river and the terrestrial habitats beyond. Each river has a variety of habitats along its banks, and this is also true of the Marteg. As you walk along its route through the reserve you will notice its borders of marshy ground, pebbly stretches, boulders strewn as if by some gigantic hand, woodland-like patches of alder, birch and ash (*Fraxinus excelsior*), green velvet cushions of moss, inviting to any self-respecting Welsh elf. The riparian habitat is characterized by the availability of water, either from the ground which soaks up some of the river waters, or from the air as the water splashes across rocks — especially over falls, or from the draining slopes of the valley sides above.

At the deep rock gorge of Ffrwd Fawr, the high humidity creates a splendid habitat for mosses and liverworts. Over a hundred different species of these primitive plants have been recorded here and on the banks just below the gorge. The Marteg valley is a superb example of the range of species which can grow in such mid-Wales conditions — conditions arising from the rock types over which the water passes and the cool, wet upland climate. Moss species such as *Isothecium holtii* and *Hyocomium armoricum* love the spray of the waterfall, bedecking the streamside boulders in a green cloak tinged with gold. A species preferring a more risky habitat on boulders in the river, liable to be covered when the river is in spate, is the feathery, green moss *Fissidens rufulus.* In the more protected crevices of bankside boulders grow a variety of liverworts. Again, few have common names but are encumbered with ones like *Saccogyne viticulosa*, *Lejeunea lamacerina* and its cousin *Lejeunea cavifolia.* Liverworts have a similar lifestyle to mosses and enjoy similar habitats, needing a damp environment to ensure that their leaves do not dry up. Liverwort literally means 'liver plant' so named because the leaves of many species (there are over 200 in Britain) resemble livers in shape.

Another aspect of the rocky gorge, and indeed much of the far bank, is its inaccessibility to sheep. The rocky ledges provide protection for sweet-scented honeysuckle (*Lonicera periclymenum*), yellow cow-wheat (*Melampyrum pratense*) and the dandelion-like flowers of the hawkweed (*Hieracium*), the latter being a favoured morsel of sheep. The cow-wheat is an interesting plant being a parasite which gets its nourishment from the roots of other plants. The prefix 'cow' means false or worthless. Neither cow-wheat nor cow-parsley are like their name-sakes in anything more than looks. The gorge shelves are important in that they are home to some uncommon species. The moss *Leucobryum juniperoideum* has only been noted once before in Radnorshire. Even more rare is the nationally uncommon wood bitter vetch (*Vicia orobus*). In 1989 only three specimens of this plant were found at Gilfach; with luck, more will flourish in the years to come.

Growing on the far banks, just down from the falls, are what appear to be large buttercups. In fact these belong to another locally uncommon species, the globeflower (*Trollius europaeus*), pretty in its yellow garb, yet poisonous. It is on this left bank, as you face downstream, that the greatest variety of bankside plants is to be found, again because they are protected from grazing. On the wetter ground grows the delicate looking lesser skullcap (*Scutellarai minor*), so-called because of its resemblance to the headgear of Roman soldiers, along with other species typical of upland, boggy areas. These include the bog asphodel (*Narthecium ossifragum*) whose spiky yellow plants were used as hair dye. Also present in abundance are the carnivorous, insect-eating sundew (*Drosera rotundifolia*) and butterwort (*Pinguicula vulgaris*).

The river is another deterrent to sheep and plants on the little islands on the stretch of river that swings away from the railway track are protected from their nibbling. Here grow water mint and primroses (*Primula vulgaris*) used to both heal wounds and keep witches away from cattle. Large clumps of marsh marigolds (*Caltha palustris*) can be seen, the buds of which can be used in cooking and pickling as a substitute for capers. On the far bank of this section, and dotted elsewhere are small areas of alder. These sections of woodland are dominated by alder but also contain other species such as birch and ash. This specialist woodland is known as alder carr and, as with all aspects of the river, is dependent on water. In

———

this case the alder need to grow near the water table where the soil is permanently wet.

The Marteg is a good example of an upland stream. Its clear waters contain life adapted for the fast lane. Along its banks, undisturbed by man or sheep, grow species you are unlikely to see elsewhere, as well as more common species. The nature reserve status of the area means that these creatures and plants have a home which will be protected for the foreseeable future.

(Left) BOG ASPHODEL – ITS LATIN NAME MEANS BONE-BREAKER.
(Right) RAVENS OVER ONE OF GILFACH'S OUTSTANDING STONE WALLS.

———

6

WILD HILLS AND
FRIENDLY FIELDS

Gilfach valley is reminiscent of an old-fashioned quilt with its patchwork of small fields, unusual in the modern landscape. Small fields made sense to the people who lived and farmed here. They provided a series of spaces that could be used on a rotating basis for a variety of purposes. Fields bounded by deep hedgerows or stone walls provided sheltered pasture for sheep, cattle and horses during the winter months. These animals fertilized the ground, making it ripe for the spring and summer growth of a wide variety of plants which were later harvested and dried to make hay, additional winter fodder for the animals.

The small farm of Gilfach is only 413 acres (167 hectares) of which one third comprises fields, 31 of them. The smallest is only an acre (0.4 hectares), the largest a mere 4.4 acres (1.8 hectares). These fields are delineated by boundaries; some hedgerows, others fences and yet others, stone walls and ditches topped by layered hedges. There are some twenty hedges at Gilfach, not all of which are in particularly good condition, a legacy of the general desertion of the site over the last thirty years. Some of the hedges at Gilfach probably date back nearly a thousand years. Stone and ditch boundaries were common in pre-Roman times and we know from the tumuli on Wyloer Hill that Gilfach has been inhabited for several thousand years. The hedges at Gilfach are known as mature, that is they contain along their length fully grown trees, left both as ornament and additional shelter by successive generations of farmers as they annually trimmed the hedge. In some places there are gaps where trees have died and the remaining hole has not been filled.

Even more than the oakwood, the hedge is home to many species of plant and anima. The hedge is a blending of the features of several habitats; being more exposed than woodland, yet more sheltered than the fields it protects. The hedge, with its tangle of branches, a mixture of nut and fruit bearing trees and shrubs, provides nest sites, hiding places and food for all sorts of creature. Beneath, in sunny spots and areas of shade, grow a multitude of flowering plants and grasses, again a veritable restaurant for insects, mammals and birds, some of which themselves are edible commodities for the various predators who live in the hedge or merely visit it to feed. In addition, the hedges act as narrow linkways in the Gilfach valley; safe corridors which animals can use as they travel over the site.

The Gilfach hedges in spring and summer are a delight, full of the colour of a cottage garden. To the knowledgeable folk who once lived here the hedgerows were not merely useful for keeping stock in, or out, of particular fields. Throughout the year the hedges were a source of fuel, food and medicine. Amongst the plants we can find here at Gilfach are some of the most beneficial, as well as some of the most poisonous.

Beneath the hedge there are several grass species, not noted for their pretty colours but interesting all the same. Goose-grass (*Galium aparine*) is not only a favourite for sheep, its young shoots are tasty in salads and its seeds can be roasted and used as a substitute for coffee. This is one of the 'cleaver' grasses, so named because of its hairy surface which allows it to cleave or stick to stems of taller plants or the clothes of passersby – no doubt why it has the additional name of 'Sticky Willie'. It has traditional medicinal uses too, being recommended for the treatment of piles, ulcers and various skin diseases including scurvy, a common complaint in days gone by when nutrition was not as good as it is now.

At the base of the hedge are a profusion of flowering plants, each making use of the protection from the wind afforded by the hedge. Here we find the maroon flowers of betony (*Stachys officinalis*), the *officinalis* part of its name indicating its formal status as a medicine accorded to it by the herbalists. Betony has been recognized for its healing properties since Roman times in the treatment of a variety of ills such as liver complaints. Its leaves, when dried, were also used for making tea and snuff. Here too we find eyebright (*Euphrasia officinalis*), known in Wales as 'Christ's eye'. This is a semi-parasitic plant which grows best when its roots are attached to those of other plants from which it takes part of its nutrients. As its name suggests, eyebright was used to assist in the healing of eye problems.

In addition to their medicinal and edible properties, plants often had religious connections. For example, the yellow flowers of St John's wort (*Hypericum perforatum*) were supposed to first appear on the saint's day. This flower was made famous by the Crusaders, the Order of St John, who took it as their emblem, possibly because of its traditional use in stopping the bleeding of wounds as well as any religious connection. Another plant used for wound healing was bugle (*Ajuga reptans*), whose small spikes of blue flowers add delicate colour to the hedge. Some plants have beneficial properties which are not so easily detected. The foxglove (*Digitalis purpurea*) whose attractive flowers give it its various names such as 'goblin's thimble' or 'fairy finger', is extremely poisonous. Yet from it comes the potent drug digitalis, used extensively in modern medicine in the treatment of heart conditions.

The rich variety of plants found along the base of the hedges, and the trees forming the hedge itself or towering above, are enjoyed by over 200 species. Bumble

bees (*Bombus*), with their long tongues, reap a harvest of nectar and in turn pollinate the flowers they visit. They are of especial importance to common toadflax (*Linaria vulgaris*) and small toadflax. These plants with their deep, snapdragon-like flowers rely on the bees for fertilization. Grasshoppers (*Chorthippus brunneus*) rasp their legs together to produce melodic sounds reminiscent of the Mediterranean. Amongst the stems are aphids, flies and gall insects, such as the bramble gall wasp (*Diastrophus rubi*) which, like the oak gall wasps in the oakwood, deposits its eggs on the leaves of the bramble. The bramble entwines its way throughout the hedge, its prickly stems adding to the boundary's effectiveness. Draped across the twigs and branches of the various shrubs are the gossamer threads of spiders' webs. Perhaps the most noticeable, as its rainbow colours shimmer with dew, is the familiar web of the common garden or orbweb spider (*Araneus diadematus*).

Feeding on the insect hordes are diverse species of bird such as tits and the tiny wren (*Troglodytes troglodytes*) which forages along the bark and amongst the ground flora in its quest for beetles, larvae, ants and spiders. Nuthatches (*Sittea europaea*) supplement their diet of nuts and acorns with various insects, whilst the hedge-sparrow (*Prunella modularis*) feasts on the hips of the wild or dog rose (*Rosa canina*), the fruits of the hawthorn (*Crataegus monogyna*) and insects too. This bird, with its unglamorous brown plumage, is not a sparrow at all. In fact it is a member of the Accentor family. It is known as a sparrow because, in the Middle Ages, that was the common name given to any small brown bird.

Mammals, too, feast on the fruits and insects of the hedgerow. Here the woodmouse lives out its secret life and the solitary hedgehog trundles through the undergrowth, its spines protecting it from the prickles of the hawthorn and bramble. We all associate the hedgehog with its spiny coat and habit of curling up in a tight ball in the presence of danger, not an effective tactic when the danger is a car. The hedgehog's upper part of its body is covered in many thousands of spines which replace the furry coat of other mammals. The spines are strong and long lasting, individual spines only being shed every year or so. They give the hedgehog good protection against predators, though injured, young and sick animals are eaten by foxes and badgers. We do not tend to associate the clockwork-toy-like gait of the hedgehog with the ability to travel long

WATER SHREW.

distances, yet a hedgehog can travel 2 miles (3 kilometres) a night in its search for insects, caterpillars and slugs, as well as a mate. Hedgehogs are not by nature noisy animals, nor do they have particularly good eyesight. But they do have keen noses, and, standing quietly alongside a hedge, or in a garden, you may hear one snuffling loudly as it frequently tests the air.

Hedgehogs tend to make several nests (hibernacula) in winter and may relocate during the warmer nights of winter and early spring, only truly emerging from their slumbers in April. The summer is taken up with the rearing of the young, a mother's chore. Four to six young are born, pink and hairless, in a grass-lined nest. Their eyes open after about a fortnight and a week later they begin to leave the nest to accompany their mother on foraging expeditions. As with the bats, cold, wet weather can cause serious problems to hedgehogs, for a reduction in the insect population can mean they are unable to put on enough fat to see them through the winter. Indeed, though a hedgehog can reach the ripe old age of seven in the wild, only 30% of them will survive their first winter.

Another member of the hedge community is that minute creature, the common shrew (*Sorex araneus*), whose size belies its strength of character. Not for nothing did Shakespeare immortalize the temperament of the beast in *The Taming of the Shrew*, not without reason is this creature associated with vindictive, nasty

'WALLS HAVE TONGUES …'

The stone walls we see rambling their way across the countryside link us through time to our early ancestors and beyond. Most of the walls we see, and certainly those at Gilfach, are constructed from local stone. As such they give us an enticing glimpse of the rocks hidden beneath the soil and vegetation. The walls at Gilfach are built from local shales which date back to the Ordovician and Silurian geological periods (see Chapter I). They tend to be retaining walls (with one side against a bank of soil) rather than the free standing ones seen in other parts of the country. A perfect example runs alongside the St Harmon road leading to the site. Like free standing walls, these too have two faces, though the inner face tends to be hidden in the earth bank.

Stone walls have been built to the same basic design, with regional variations, since Neolithic man first began to change from a hunter-gatherer existence to a pastoral lifestyle, some 6,000 years ago. Throughout much of England many of our stone walls are far more recent, some dating from the Middle Ages, and a large percentage from the time of the Enclosures, between the late 18th and mid-19th centuries, when land was partitioned off by large landowners to their own profit. However, here in mid-Wales during these later periods hedges were preferred over stone walls, because the local shales are extremely fissile, that is they have a tendency to split easily and as such are not terribly useful for a freestanding wall; a hedge is a better bet. The design of the walls you see at Gilfach reflect this tendency to split. They do not have top stones, but are built from large stone slabs set vertically, if somewhat haphazardly, into the ground, banked with earth and, in some cases topped with a hedge for good measure.

While Gilfach's walls are likely to have been built in recent centuries, the lines they follow may well be of prehistoric origin, a surmise supported both by the

curving nature of their design and by the prehistoric tumulus present on the southern slope of Wyloer Hill near the road. The walls and hedges bound small fields near the farmstead. The fields were small and entailed a lot of hard work. The large slabs of stone had to be quarried nearby and manually transported to their place in the wall; no easy feat. The small enclosures are known as 'infields' and were used to cultivate crops and hay, sheep being grazed on them during parts of the year in order to fertilize the soil. The outfields, that is anything not so enclosed, was used as rough pasture just as it is today. The walls and hedges of Gilfach make it seem like a tiny island of cultivation and civilization, surrounded by a sea of wild moorland.

Many stone walls, like hedges, have been destroyed in recent times. Like hedges, they need maintaining and are labour intensive, a characteristic opposed to our modern way of thinking. Indeed, a few decades ago the skill of drystone wall building had all but vanished. However, it is now enjoying a renaissance, especially with people interested in conservation such as the members of the British Trust of Conservation Volunteers who have been instrumental in the repair of old walls and building of new ones on several sites, including Gilfach. But why should we bother to preserve them? Well, first is that they are part of our heritage, an integral feature in the landscape we call the British countryside. Second, whilst they may appear to be rather barren of life, they do play an important role in the lives of many species. All walls are of use to a variety of plants and animals, and those comprising stone faced banks, especially if surmounted by a hedge-type layer of shrubs are of particular importance - like those at Gilfach.

So, what sort of habitat is a stone wall? Different walls can provide radically different habitats. For example, the walls here at Gilfach are built from acidic stone and thus are quite different from those built from more alkaline

habits. Indeed, the Latin name for this creature, *araneus*, means 'of spiders' and refers to the traditional belief that this ferocious beast was poisonous.

The shrew swiftly bustles about using its long snout to explore and probe the vegetation for any insect it can find. Whilst it will eat almost anything it does not particularly relish slugs. It needs to be efficient as it only has a tiny body and a high metabolic rate which means it uses a lot of energy. A shrew weighs approxi-

---

rocks such as limestone. Though the range of animal and plant species that inhabit a stone wall environment is limited, this does not reduce their value.

Walls in general are particularly well drained habitats, though those backed by earth banks are less so. More important, perhaps, is the aspect of the wall. The south face of a wall can be very dry and warm during the summer, giving almost desert-like conditions, while the north face stays cool and moist. Walls are particularly important for lichens, mosses and ferns, the lichens preferring the dry southern sides and the mosses and ferns the northern aspect, a similar distribution to that we find on the tree trunks in the oakwood. Walls provide essential habitats for rock dwelling saxicolous species, such as navelwort (*Umbilicus rupestris*), in areas where there are few, if any natural rocks exposed. In essence, the walls at Gilfach provide an extension of the scree outcrops of Wyloer Hill. In terms of conservation importance, it has been suggested that the loss of stone walls would be even more serious in botanical terms than the loss of hedgerows, especially in the intensively farmed lowlands of Britain where natural habitats are few. This is because the rock-loving plants so threatened are often slow growing and difficult to establish, nor would they have recourse to other alternative habitats such as woodland or gardens tended by sympathetic gardeners.

Walls are not just of importance to plants, many animals make use of them too. Spiders and insects make homes in the dry parts of the wall, tucking themselves in the multitudinous nooks and crannies. This means that the walls are good feeding sites for insect eaters. Reptiles such as the slow-worm found in mid-Wales can take shelter in the warmth of the wall. Indeed, banks and walls are virtually the only places where many such animals can safely and warmly overwinter. Birds and mammals also use the walls. The tiny wheatear, with its distinctive white tail (its name comes from the Old English 'white arse'), sparrows, flycatchers and others all use walls as nest sites. Small mammals such as voles, mice and rats can all seek safety in the gaps provided by the stones. Some may use the wall as a protected highway as they travel from one area of the site to another, others may construct their homes in, or beneath the wall. Indeed, rabbits and rats can run riot in the tunnels they construct in the earth banks, potentially causing havoc to the wall's foundations. All this life means the walls are attractive hunting grounds for polecats and their cousins, while foxes may do further damage as they dig into the bank in their quest for a tasty meal. It not just the small creatures which use the wall, many a sheep and human has lain down to take advantage of the shelter from the wind provided by the labour of our forebears.

> With aching hands and bleeding feet
> We dig and heap, lay stone on stone
> We bear the burden and the heat
>
> Matthew Arnold ('Morality')

mately 10 grammes (0.3 ounces) and feeds every 2-3 hours, night and day, needing to eat 70% of its body weight every 24 hours. For a human, this would mean consuming some 40 kilos (89 lb) of food each day. With its sensitive nose and acute sense of smell, the shrew can even find dormant insects buried 12 centimetres (5 inches) deep in the soil. It attacks the head of its prey, proceeding to munch its way downwards from the head, discarding large wings, legs and other unpalatable bits. Given that insects tend themselves to be 70% water (as indeed are we), a shrew needs to eat some 100 maggot-sized insects every day just to survive. This is a formidable task, and shrew populations tend to crash during hard winters. But in a well established, well maintained hedge there is a good supply of insects, some 1,000 or more for every square metre (1.2 square yards).

The shrew gets its reputation for its bad temper from its social life, or rather its lack of social life. Basically solitary animals they only meet each other civilly to mate. The rest of the time they are extremely territorial, ferociously defending their land from their neighbours. The meeting of two individuals can be clearly heard as they scream abuse at each other, each more than willing to engage in a fight. Even young shrews, born blind and naked, soon grow and within 25 days of birth are no longer tolerant of their brothers and sisters but become aggressive and disperse to find their own homes. These youngsters will breed themselves the following summer, but it is an aged shrew who lives more than a year.

Hedgerows are important refuges for nesting birds such as the wren. The wren was once regarded as the king of birds, and anyone who harmed it was believed to suffer a terrible fate. With its cocky turned-up tail and penetrating song, this is a delightfully dainty bird, captivatingly depicted on the now obsolete farthing coin. Deep in the hedgerow, it builds its dome-shaped nest of mosses, leaves and grasses. It will also take happily to using bird-boxes in which it lays its white eggs delicately mottled with red-brown spots. The wren is sensitive to cold weather and will gather together to keep warm, as many as forty having been found cuddled up in a single nest box – cosy if somewhat crowded.

The decorative goldfinch (*Carduelis carduelis*) with its red face, yellow wings and bands of white and black was once a favourite cage bird, caught for its enchanting, liquid song. Towards the end of the last century so great was the trade that the goldfinch population had been brought close to extinction. The saving of this bird was one of the first tasks of the, then, Society for the Protection of Birds (now the Royal Society for the Protection of Birds). It uses the hedgerows as safe

DUNNOCK AND PRIMROSE.

nesting sites, but can be seen as it feeds in groups, known as charms, on the seeds of the flowers of the Gilfach fields. It is especially partial to the downy seed-heads of the thistle (*Cirsium vulgare*).

Also living in the hedge, or rather under it, are rabbits (*Oryctolagus cuniculus*); these too venture out to feed in the fields. Best seen in the early evening or morning, these herbivores can do extensive damage to crops and are the bane of many a farmer. Attempts to eradicate them in the 1950s with the introduction of myxomatosis did not succeed and in many parts of the country they are a serious pest. For all that, I have to confess a love of these timid, gentle beasts. They too have a role to play in Gilfach's web of life. Along with the sheep they graze the land, keeping the sward short and thus suitable for many smaller plants. Along with small birds, insects and other mammals, rabbits provide a tasty meal for buzzards, goshawks and the beautiful red kite. This latter bird, regal in its rich auburn plumage, was once common throughout the country. However, it is now rare, confined to the remote hills of this part of mid-Wales, having fallen foul of hunters and the cumulative effects of pesticides. Though they do not yet nest in Gilfach, they may be seen over the site seeming to circle tirelessly and effortlessly.

Roughly, the fields at Gilfach can be divided into two major groups, those that are basically dry and those which, for most of the year, are waterlogged to some degree. Within this division is a further category, that of improved and unimproved pasture. Improved pasture is a modern phenomenon and means pasture that has been treated with herbicides to get rid of unwanted plants, pesticides to kill insects, fertilizer to improve the nutrient quality of the ground, lime to reduce the acidity of the soil; it has often also been drained. Improved pasture tends to be a poor habitat for wildlife, dominated here at Gilfach by rye-grass (*Lollium perenne*). However, from the farmer's point of view it makes excellent grazing for sheep, the rich sward enabling lambs to grow rapidly, obtaining its goodness indirectly from the milk of their dams and directly by eating it. Ecologically, though, these dark green fields are of little importance. Approximately a quarter of the pastures on the site are so improved, but Gilfach's real quality lies in its unimproved land.

Unimproved pasture in contrast can be home to a hundred or more different species of plant, many of which can be found at Gilfach. These are cut every summer and dried in the sun, gathered as hay to provide sweet and nutritious feed for the animals in winter. They also provide a refuge and food supply for many wild creatures.

The fields near the river tend to be damp and even waterlogged in parts known as 'flushes'. Flushes are where the water table reaches the surface and can easily be distinguished by the rich, deep greens of the flora growing on them. It is here that the rushes and sedges grow, used by previous inhabitants for lights, basket making and even bedding. At first glance these plants look similar but are easily distinguished by remembering that 'sedges have edges and rushes are round'. This refers to the shape of the stem which in the case of sedges is square or triangular. There are at least nine species of sedge and five of rushes found at Gilfach. The soft-rush (*Juncus effusus*) was favoured for the making of rushlights because of its pithy stem. It grows in tussocks with its dull brown flowers relying on the wind for fertilization and seed dispersal. All of the rushes and sedges depend on the wind for this part of their lifecycle and thus do not need to attract insects and other animals with bright flowers and sweet scents. They also have tough stems, making them somewhat unpalatable to grazing animals.

Another dweller of the damp pastures is marsh lousewort (*Pedicularis palustris*) so named because it was believed to produce lice which infest the wool of sheep. Although sheep-lice (*Trichodectes sphaerocephalus*) are also found in these wet pastures, they do not have any connection with marsh lousewort. Growing prostrate along the ground is marsh pennywort (*Hydrocotyle vulgaris*), whose tiny, greenish-white flowers elude the gaze of the casual passerby. This plant too was disliked by the shepherd, believed to cause liver disease in sheep, the real culprit being the damp-loving liver fluke which the sheep ingest when grazing infected pasture. Rising tall above all are the bright flowers of yellow flag (*Iris psuedacorus*) whose leaves are so sharply edged that they can cut the hands of the careless gatherer. Many of these water loving plants have cousins in drier areas of Gilfach, for example marsh bedstraw (*Gallium palustre*) is related to lady's bedstraw and marsh St John's wort (*Hypericum elodes*) to the St John's wort growing in the hedgerow.

Amongst the damp flora of the these meadows are animals who need water in which to breed. Common frogs (*Rana temporaria*) lay approximately a thousand eggs each in pools of still water; at Gilfach they use puddles and marshy areas, not the rapid waters of the Marteg. The tiny froglets range into the lush, damp pastures. These amphibia hibernate in the winter in muddy ditches or crevices in old walls, but in the spring and summer are typically found in meadows. Having a visual system designed for detecting tiny movements, customized bug detectors and rapid reflexes the frog captures insects on its sticky tongue. It is particularly active at dusk, having raised its body temperature by basking in the sun. It rests and hunts near cover, for the frog has many enemies, forming part of the diet of many animals we see at Gilfach, including kites, buzzards, otters, herons, owls, crows and badger.

Such predators also hunt over the drier pastures, away from the river. These fields gently creep up the slope of the hill, the tilt of the land draining away the rain. It is here that the rabbit, who definitely does not like having its feet wet, comes out to feed, frolic and mate. For the rabbit, death may even come within the 'safety' of the burrow, in the form of polecats, weasels and stoats. Rabbits represent a substantial meal nicely packaged in a single individual. Consequently, they are worth hunting. All this means that rabbits have to be vigilant as they graze the meadow or hillside. Rabbits have extremely good senses of sight, hearing and smell all tuned to detecting the merest wingbeat, rustle of grass or hint of scent which may indicate the approach of a predator. When grazing a rabbit repeatedly interrupts its meal to sit up and survey its surroundings. The further it is away from its burrow, the more frequently it stops eating to look out for its enemies. Naturally, two sets of eyes (or ears or noses) are better than one, and the rabbit makes full use of this maxim by living in social groups. If there are other rabbits around, an individual can spend more time feeding and less time looking about. It can rely, to some extent, on the vigilance of the other rabbits to warn it of any approaching danger. Any rabbit suspecting danger will thump the ground hard with its hind feet, thereby warning its fellows. Also, a fleeing rabbit sticks up its tail, displaying the white underside as a warning flag. Animals also pick up signals from other species, for example excited chatter from disturbed small birds will instantly put the rabbits on the alert.

Rabbits tend to be out and about from early evening through to dawn, as are many of their enemies, not least Brock the badger. This powerfully built animal is an opportunistic feeder eating a variety of foodstuffs including earthworms, fruit, acorns, insects, woodmice, shrews and rabbits. Badgers (*Meles Meles*) are rather short-sighted and not terribly fast movers, though they can attain speeds of 19 miles an hour (30 kilometres an hour) when pushed. Their normal lumbering gait means they usually are restricted to eating rabbits that are injured or incapacitated through disease such as myxomatosis. Badgers also dig out baby rabbits from the shallow nest burrows. Badgers too live in burrows called setts. These they share with 5 or 6 other badgers and may also share their home with a variety of other creatures, including foxes, rabbits, woodmice and polecats. Handy homes for these other creatures, as the badgers have done all the hard excavation work! In a way the badger epitomises the intricate connections of a natural community. It shares its home with other animals, some of whom may even form part of its diet. It also makes full use of a site such as Gilfach, foraging in the meadows, along the hedges, in the wood, acting both as a herbivore and carnivore.

RINGLET BUTTERFLY ON RAGWORT.

The badger has been immortalized in *Wind in the Willows*, and for me was a childhood favourite, peering over the top of his glasses, giving firm and friendly advice to the irrepressible Toad. The badger has little to fear from other creatures in the countryside, except the most aggressive creature of all, namely ourselves. Although fully protected by the law, badgers are still ruthlessly perse-

DUNNOCK.

cuted. They are illegally poisoned with gas in their setts, caught in snares, shot at night or dug out and used as live bait for dogs who are set on the badger to kill it in the name of sport. Others are accidentally killed on roads, though planners now tend to incorporate underground badger routes should a new road cross established badger paths. In some parts of the country these delightful creatures are scarce in number. The best we can do for them is help conserve or re-create appropriate habitats, and then leave them to their own devices. This would mean that we could indulge ourselves with getting permission from the landowner to watch their antics, and I cannot think of a more delightful way of entering the hidden world of nature which surrounds us.

Scurrying throughout the dry meadows, with an air of being on errands of great importance, are ants, ants and more ants. There are over forty different species in Britain, but most obvious here at Gilfach are the yellow meadow ants (*Lasius flavus*). These excavate away into the soil, building an intricate maze of tunnels in which their multitudes live sheltered from the worst of the weather. These colony homes will last for over fifty years. The ants' tunnelling activities

BADGERS EMERGING FROM THEIR SETT.

result in small mounds of earth being thrown up all over the meadows. These mounds tend to be covered in grass and are not as large or conspicuous as those produced by moles (*Talpa europaea*), which also bore through the meadows of Gilfach. Both mole hills and ant hills serve to till the soil and provide lookout posts for rabbits. Rabbits use the mounds as latrines, the faeces deposited at these sites act to inform other rabbits of territorial boundaries. In addition, the rabbit's droppings fertilize the soil and there is often a profusion of plant growth around the mounds. The ants themselves are herders and harvesters, living a life analogous to that of the former human inhabitants of Gilfach: they herd aphids (*Aphididae*) taking them out to graze in the spring and milking them of the sticky substances they produce. In the colder weather, they tend the aphid larvae underground. Further, the ants harvest vegetative matter and nectar as additional food sources.

In addition to their farming activities, ants are efficient detritivores, helping to clear the pasture of faeces and dead animals. Many fungi also take part in the decomposition process, part of nature's refuse collection community. Fungi grow all over Gilfach, but the greatest variety are to be found in the pastures. Here I would like to just give you a taste, or perhaps not, of the beauty of these primitive plants. For *beware*, many fungi look appetizing and even resemble those available in the shops, but these can be misleading for several are poisonous. Apart from the fact that Gilfach is a nature reserve and plants should not be picked, it is never a good idea to pick or eat fungi without recourse to expert advice on identification.

Several edible forms of fungi grow at Gilfach including the field and the similar looking horse mushroom (*Agaricus arvensis*), and its larger cousin, *Agaricus macrosporus*, which can have a cap of 25 centimetres (10 inches) in diameter, but has no common name. Another country table delight is the puffball of which three species grow at Gilfach, *Bovista plumbea*, *Bovista nigrescens* and *Vascellum pratense*. These species range in size from approximately 2-6 centimetres (1-2.5 inches) whilst the giant puffball (*Calvatia gigantae*), which does not grow here can reach 30 centimetres (12 inches) in diameter. The fungi we see are the fruits of the plant and the seeds are known as 'spores'. Puffballs are so named because when the spores are ripe the puffball starts to dry out, breaking the thin filaments attaching them to the ground. This means the puffball is free to blow around, becoming knocked about and finally splitting open releasing the spores to the wind for dispersal. A single giant puffball can release some seven thousand billion spores, that is a lot of baby fungi. But as with all things in nature many do not survive.

Scattered across the meadows are parasol mushrooms (*Lepiota procera*), looking rather like drab brown, scaly, open umbrellas, hence their name. These can grow to a considerable height of some 30 centimetres (12 inches), some of the tallest fungi in Britain. They appear throughout the late summer and autumn, from August to October. They are relished for their nutty taste, a reputation no doubt enhanced by their scarcity – it is just as well that they are free to grow in safety here at Gilfach.

Similar in shape, having an upright stem and flat cap, are the fly agaric (*Amanita muscaria*) fungi. Their bright scarlet colour clearly sends out a powerful warning of their lethal character. Yet at the same time they are favourite of children's stories. Their caps are covered with white splodges, seemingly stuck on by fairy folk. Though toxic, in minor doses these fungi have hallucinatory properties, possibly why Lewis Carroll depicted his hookah-smoking caterpillar of *Alice in Wonderland* fame sitting on one of them. The fly agaric also has intoxicating properties, not only for people but also for flies. Flies are attracted to a bait, a dish of milk, in which the fungi is soaking. As the flies take the bait they become stupefied by the fungi. They were not the only ones to be so mentally dulled. Lapplanders used to

PARASOL MUSHROOM.

feed the fungi to their reindeer, and then brewed a potent, inebriating drink from the reindeers' urine … I am not sure this will ever catch on with the cocktail set!

Gilfach's finest fungi are surely the wax caps, and of these the pride of place goes to the parrot fungus (*Hygrocybe psittacina*). This can occur in a rainbow of colours. Individuals may be bright green, orange, yellow or even a delicate shade of pink. They appear waxy, especially when damp, when they become slimy to touch.

There are many other sources of colour in these unimproved, dry pastures. A host of flowering plants bespangle the old hay meadows, especially in high summer. Over a hundred different species of plant can be found, compared to the paucity of species that grow in the artificially treated, improved pastures which now dominate the landscape. Some of the plants found here at Gilfach are of both local and national importance,

FLY AGARIC.

MOUNTAIN
PANSY.

so rare have they become. In the pastures there are several which are officially considered as locally uncommon. This means that they are at risk and without due care will become rare or even extinct in an area which was once a stronghold for that species. One such plant is the decorative, mountain pansy (*Viola lutea*). This ground hugging plant would, under ideal circumstances, form small mats of colour. However, as its uncommon status indicates, sadly it does not grow in any profusion. Many individual plants which are grazed adopt a flat, rosette posture growing close to the ground in response to having been nibbled, an attempt to avoid being nibbled in the future. The same plant if growing unexposed to repetitive nibbling will be taller and more upright, as you can see at Gilfach, with ribwort plantain (*Plantago lanceolata*) and bird's foot trefoil (*Lotus corniculatus*).

Whilst you will have to search near the soil for the pansy, a hunt for dyer's greenweed (*Genista tinctoria*) will not incur backache. A member of the broom family, this plant grows up to 60 centimetres (24 inches) high, waving its bright yellow flags almost as a tribute to the summer sun. As its name suggests, this plant was used widely for dyeing clothes. A third, though not the last, member of Gilfach's 'locally uncommon gang' is the harebell (*Campanula rotundifolia*). A beautiful and elegant plant, with its cluster of heart-shaped leaves at the base from which emerges a tall delicate stem, fringed with slender green leaves and crowned with a cluster of lilac-blue, bell-shaped flowers. A cousin of the bluebell but somewhat more graceful and can be substantially taller reaching a height of 50 centimetres (20 inches).

Some plants that are common at Gilfach are under threat elsewhere, for example Devil's-bit scabious (*Succisa pratensis*). That eminent 17th-century herbalist, Culpeper, highly recommended this plant as a cure for illnesses associated with the powers of evil, such as plague and snake bites. Obviously, a plant so capable of undoing the Devil's work would certainly be an annoyance to him and it is from this that the plant gets its name. The tap root, the main thick root, of the

SKIPPER ON SCABIOUS.

Devil's- bit scabious is not pointed as it is in other plants but looks as if it has been bitten off. This was considered to be the work of the Devil in his attempt to kill the plant.

A hay meadow must be a butterfly's delight, the range of flowering plants all producing their own unique nectars to be sipped. Not least of these is the thistle, standing to attention in its purple-topped, prickly armour. The dark green fritillary (*Argynnis aglaia*) has a special penchant for the thistle flowers, and helps fertilize them as it partakes of their sweet nectar. For this the goldfinch should be grateful because, as we know, this bird is rather partial to the resulting thistle seeds. As you wander through Gilfach in July and August, you may see this butterfly perched on the thistle tops.

Caterpillars do not tend to eat the same plants as the adult butterflies; and caterpillars tend to be restricted in range of plant. So the presence of the adult butterfly indicates the presence of the plants needed to feed the caterpillar stage. For example, the dark green fritillary butterfly indicates the presence of dog violets (*Viola canina*), on which its caterpillars exclusively eat. The caterpillar of the green-veined white butterfly (*Pieris napi*) must have Mediterranean connections given its partiality for Jack-by-the-hedge (*Alliaria petiolata*) which has a strong garlic flavour.

The small skipper butterfly (*Thymelicus sylvestris*) has a liking for the grasses of damp places, be they in the meadows, near the river, or on the hillside. In contrast, a more shade-loving species is the sombre-looking ringlet butterfly (*Aphantopus hyperantus*) which is found on the edge of the oakwood and along the hedgerows. A butterfly which ranges from the valley bottom to top of Wyloer Hill is the small heath (*Coenonympha pamphilus*), attracted by the rough meadows for feeding it rests on the taller grasses and rushes.

Wyloer Hill dominates the Gilfach site, its rocky eastern face overlooking the farmstead whilst its sunny, southern slopes contrast with the deep, shady greens of the Gamallt plantation opposite. These two slopes of Wyloer are owned by the Radnorshire Wildlife Trust and rise up to 412 metres (1,351 feet) above sea level. In summer they are alluring, in winter bleak.

As we climb up Wyloer we traverse the lower slopes covered in a carpet of bracken (*Pteridium aquilinum*), patterned with scattered hawthorn bushes. Bracken is a member of the fern family, but unusual in that it grows in continuously spreading communities on upland hillsides. These are so dense that they restrict the

' … AND HEDGES EARS'

If, as the poet Swift suggested, hedges do indeed have ears, then there is much of our history to which they have been party. Hedges have been wending their way over hill and dale for a thousand years or more and are one of our oldest artefacts. The study of hedges can reveal much about the lives of our ancestors, the layout of their homesteads and communities. They are also extremely important to our wildlife, regular little nature reserves in their own right.

The creation of a hedge is a skill which recently is enjoying a resurgence as those concerned with conservation attempt to look after this aspect of our heritage. Many hedges are based on hawthorn; a highly successful hedging plant. First a bank is built up which will provide the drained soil in which the hedge will grow. Into the face of this bank are planted saplings of live hawthorn about 20 centimetres (8 inches) apart. These uprights are known as 'plashers'. When the plashers are a reasonable size, they are cut diagonally near the base leaving a 'lamb's tongue width' still attached to the root. This cut stem is bent over to the right at an angle of about 30°, thus forming the layered barrier. Between the plashers are planted upright stakes at about metre (yard) intervals. The plashers are then woven between these uprights. The whole thing is held in place by criss-crossing thin hazel rods (obtained from coppiced trees) along the tops of the uprights. Both the plashers and uprights will grow into a thick barrier. Sapling trees such as oak can be incorporated into the hedge as uprights, or may grow naturally from seed. Other plants such as bramble and honeysuckle are often wound through along with the plashers, serving to keep out animals whilst the hawthorn becomes established.

Hedges need to be maintained and trimmed on an annual basis. For young hedges this needs to be done with care, by hand. Mechanical trimmers are used on mature hedges, but even then they can do a lot of damage as they indiscriminately flail the hedge tops, leaving the plant battered and removing the tops of any trees which are attempting to grow through. Every decade or two, the hedge needs an overhaul, for example parts will need to be relaid as gaps occur; as is the situation at Gilfach. Left alone, a hedge will eventually become a line of trees, for the art of hedge laying is to fool nature by making trees grow horizontally rather than vertically.

Over 1,000 species of plant, half of the species of native mammals, a fifth of our bird species and all of our reptiles can be found in hedgerows. Many are highly dependent on this habitat and are now becoming rare with the removal of the hedges. As hedges mature, so they become home to a greater variety of plant species and this can be used to date them. If you walk along a 30-metre (100-foot) stretch of hedge and count the number of tree species, you can make a rough estimate of the age of that hedge by calculating that each species has taken 100 years to establish itself. Thus a length of hedge containing 5 species of tree is likely to be 500 years old – naturally, this is only true where the hedge is mixed, not of hedges of a single species or where management has removed all others – a good example being yew hedges in churchyards.

Whilst British hedges can date from Saxon times, many are only a couple of hundred years old, dating from the Enclosure Acts of 1760-70 and 1790-1815. Prior to these acts, hedges predominantly functioned as village boundaries and to protect croplands from grazing animals. The parliamentary Enclosure Acts served to enclose common arable and grazing land, turning over to the hands of the 'landowner' what had been, for centuries, available to all. This apportioning of the land meant that many thousands of miles of hedgerow were planted to delineate the borders of private land. With it came the opportunity for many species to colonize this extensive new habitat.

Hedges are slowly being recognized as an important part of our heritage. Yet economics tend to win over aesthetics and nature. Still we continue to destroy our heritage, with over 60% of hedgerows having been removed since 1945. Hedges are expensive. It has been reckoned that the annual cost of maintaining 22.5 kilometres (14 miles) of hedge is £4,000 and a 4 hectare (10 acre) field will be bounded by 0.8 kilometres (0.5 miles) of hedge. Yet hedges are important both aesthetically and historically, as indeed are buildings such as our magnificent medieval cathedrals which are of a similar age to many of our hedgerows. We would be outraged at the loss of one of these glorious buildings. Perhaps we should be just as outraged at the loss of these medieval monuments of the countryside!

DARK GREEN FRITILLARY ON THISTLE IN HAY MEADOW.

growth of other plants, often to the point of total exclusion. Further, it is poison-ous when eaten in any quantity and is usually avoided by cattle and sheep. It would be an understatement to say that bracken is a problem in our uplands. This plant spreads via its roots, creeping rootstocks sending up shoots away from the mother plant. Because it spreads underground, bracken is extremely difficult to eradicate. In an attempt to try to keep it under control, farmers used to beat the bracken back every autumn, destroying that year's surface growth; they also used to cut it for bedding for animals. This is no longer a part of the farming calendar, particu-larly as many farms have been abandoned due to economics, especially in the more remote regions of Scotland and Wales. As a consequence, the bracken inva-sion poses a serious threat to our upland heritage.

Above the bracken the sheep survive mostly on grass species. Grasses have evolved to be able to cope with constant grazing as, unlike most plants whose growing point is at the tip of the plant, grasses grow from the bottom upwards. Grasses are analogous to icebergs, with the greenery we see above being approxi-

---

mately one tenth of the plant, the remainder being a mass of roots. These roots are extremely efficient factories, retrieving nutrients from the soil and turning them into lush green leaves. On Wyloer typical upland grass species can be found, such as sheep's fescue (*Festuca ovina*), brown bent (*Agrostis montana*), mat grass (*Nardus stricta*) and wavy hair-grass (*Deschampsia flexuosa*), so called because it looks as though someone has softly permed its delicate hair-like stem. Perhaps the most noticeable grass of these hills is purple moor grass (*Molinia caerulea*), particularly in autumn when it casts off the green coat of the hill, dressing it instead in mellow amber. This grass grows in large tussocks, its tiny purple flowers blooming from July to September. A major characteristic of this plant is that it is the only grass species on these hills which is deciduous, and loses its leaves in autumn. These are the wisps of hay one can see hanging from fence and hedge as they are buffeted about by the wind. It is this mixture of grasses that are harvested and dried to make a reasonable quality 'Rhos' hay, the Welsh word '*rhos*' meaning 'moor'.

Sheep are efficient lawnmowers, as my family can testify when I had a pet sheep for many years and the mechanical lawnmower was rarely heard. A single ewe and her lamb can munch their way through 20 kilogrammes (44 pounds) of fresh plant matter every day! This requirement means that on low quality pastures, such as Wyloer Hill, farmers are unable to graze as many sheep per hectare

RED GROUSE, TYPICAL OF THE CAMBRIAN PLATEAU.

---

as do farmers in the rich pastures of lowland Britain. In these upland, unimproved pastures sheep are kept at a density of about 2.4 per acre(1 per hectare).

The plant community we see on Wyloer has changed little over the last 500 years or more. For all of this time it is likely that Wyloer has been grazed by sheep. The major difference between now and then is the recent encroachment of bracken. Two other factors ensure that things remain the same: first is the adaptation of the plant species present to the local conditions of geology, soil type, rainfall and general weather conditions. Second is the 'sheep factor'. Sheep are selective and are partial to young, tasty plants. Thus, new plant species entering the area are likely to be highly palatable and attractive to sheep. This means their chance of establishing themselves in any great number is low.

As the sheep and rabbits, moles and voles and other creatures forage their way across Gilfach's pastures and slopes, so they litter the ground with nutrient-rich faeces. Sheep and rabbit dung is easily spotted, but you may not realize that it is home to yet another group of creatures besides the ants. These are the scarab, or dor, beetles (*Scarabaeoidea*), held sacred in Ancient Egypt, and not without good reason. Were it not for these beetles, we would be ankle deep in muck. Some species prefer cattle dung but the Minotaur beetle (*Typhaers typhoeus*) has a liking for sheep and rabbit droppings. It works in pairs, with the female doing most of the hard labour, excavating shafts under the dung. It then hauls the pellets below ground and lays its eggs. The adults as well as the larvae eat the dung, but they tend to bury far more than they need. This is an extremely useful service, for, as well as removing the dung from the surface, it also speeds up the decomposition process and the return to the soil of the nutrients locked up in the faeces.

The dor beetle works in good weather and bad. In wet weather most of the rain drains off the hillsides down to the valley below. But some collects in the hollows, gullies and clefts as well as on the flatter tops. These considerably wetter patches are called 'upland acid flushes'. The 'upland' describes their location and term 'flush' relates to the plentiful supply of water trapped in these spots. The word 'acid' refers to the nature of the water, which can be as tart as vinegar, drawing its acidity from the soil and semi-decomposed vegetation. These flushes create their own micro-habitats within the grander scene of the hill. The sight of common cotton-grass (*Eriophorum angustifolium*) is a good sign that you are approaching one of these flushes, and are likely to get extremely wet feet or caught in a bog. This tall plant reaches 75 centimetres (30 inches) in height and is

MINOTAUR
BEETLE.

not a grass at all, but a sedge which, like its cousins in the valley, grows best in wet areas. Between May and July the cotton grass is easily identified by its clusters of white, downy, fruiting bodies which look as if Peter Rabbit and friends have hung their freshly-washed tails out to dry. The cotton grass is often surrounded by a cushion of sphagnum moss (*Sphagnum*). There are a variety of species, ranging in colour from dark reds, emerald greens to bright yellow-green. These mosses act like sponges, soaking up and trapping water. Indeed this absorbent property was exploited for wiping bleeding wounds, in the same way as we might use cotton wool today.

In these flushes also grow carnivorous plants, plants that derive their nutrition from the sun and soil, but supplement the nitrogen in their diet with meat in the form of insects. Here at Gilfach grow sundew (*Drosera rotundifolia*) and butterwort (*Pinguicula vulgaris*). The former has small white flowers and the latter violet ones. Both trap unwary insects on their sticky leaves which then curl over the poor creature, holding it prisoner. The plant then releases juices which kill and digest the insect, a slow and unpleasant death.

Covering much of the eastern flank of Wyloer is heather moor with bilberry. This is a carpet of slow-growing, woody plants which remain low in height, sheltering beneath the snow in winter. In the summer the heather adds to the sweet smell and colour of the moorland, providing food for many and nest sites for the shy skylark (*Alauda arvensis*). In the autumn the bilberry provides a gourmet feast in the form of its purple-blue berries. So popular are these that the train used to stop at Marteg Bridge, disgorging day trippers from Rhayader who came to pick them for jam and pie making.

As you ascend Wyloer, you will come across outcrops of rock, especially on the junction between the southerly and easterly facing slopes. Whilst you may regard these as obstacles in your path, they are worth a closer look. On these rocks grow some hundred different species of sun-loving lichens, several of which are now rare; *Galoplaca sudpallida* is unknown elsewhere in mid-Wales. Others are now scarce throughout the country including *Umbilicaria deusta* and *Fuccidea recensa*. Lichens tend to be known only by Latin names, being rather difficult to distinguish. One, however, you will be able to spot is the aptly named bloodspot lichen (*Haematomma ventuosum*) — a patch of rust red spots on a background of green-grey clinging to the rock face.

DOR BEETLE.

———

From the top of Wyloer Hill, Gilfach is an open book spread out below — the pattern of the fields, with railway and river, the house tucked in the shelter of the hills, the oakwood contrasting with the plantation on the other side. Above you are the skylark and the wheeling buzzard. Beneath you are the rocks, the foundation of all you see.

SUNDEW – A MEAT-EATING PLANT.

———

SILLY AS SHEEP

The humble sheep has been the mainstay of man's existence for many thousands of years. In his early existence as a hunter-gatherer, man followed the wild flocks as they traversed their native habitats of open rolling mountains and slopes of the foothills.

The behaviour of sheep make them an animal admirably suited to domestication. Their natural habitat is a harsh mountainous environment where food is scarce and of low quality. Thus survival is primarily a task of finding enough to eat, rather than needing to make a swift escape from predators. Wild sheep therefore are not as nervous, nor run so fast as other potential domesticates, such as deer. Sheep provided early man with a source of food which could be easily followed and preyed upon when required.

Wild sheep are perhaps the easiest of all animals to tame, a virtue we have not been slow to exploit. This arises from the sheep's social structure. Sheep and man share aspects of their social system, a characteristic which has been important in our relationship with all of our domesticated species (with the exception of the cat). Both have a social system that is based on a single dominant leader and have home ranges across which they travel in search of food. These characteristics make them predisposed to follow a herdsman as he travels in search of food for his flock. Such a lifestyle, common to early pastoral society, can still be seen today in many parts of the world.

Because sheep are not territorial they are able to be kept in compact groups containing both sexes. Thus, they can easily be constrained with a fence or hedge, or trained to stay close to a farmstead or village, as their natural home range is quite small and localized. This is an aspect of behaviour made use of in these Welsh hills. Unlike farms of the lowlands, where sheep tend to be enclosed, the sheep here are left to wander the hillsides, in what is known as hefted flocks. These sheep tend to keep to the area in which they were born. It is fascinating to watch sheep which have been gathered from several hills, for shearing or dipping, being let loose again. As if directed by a choreographer, they stream out of the gate and peel off unerringly to their own hillside, a dance per-formed to the tat-tat of their hooves and melancholic tune of their bleatings.

There are over 200 different breeds of domestic sheep (*Ovis aries*) in the world today. Their ancestor was probably the Asiatic mouflon (*Ovis orientalis*), with the European mouflon (*Ovis musimon*) being the first domestic sheep taken to Europe by Neolithic farmers some 9, 000 years ago. This stately animal, with its large curving horns, now lives wild in the mountains of Corsica and Sardinia. Man's selective breeding of sheep has had a variety of effects on the body size, meat to fat ratios, horns and wool. Such changes were well established 8, 000 years ago. Domestic breeds tend to be shorter and to carry more fat. A lack of horns in female sheep is rare among wild sheep, but common amongst domestic breeds, including primitive breeds such as the European mouflon and Soay sheep. Perhaps the most important change is that wrought on the fleece. Wild sheep have a short woolly, undercoat covered in an outer layer of stiff hairs, called 'kemp'. Both wild and primitive domestic breeds shed the undercoat each spring, the wool being gathered from the ground or plucked from the animal. In highly domesticated breeds the kemp is absent and the wool grows throughout the year and needs to be clipped. This has the major advantage that the wool is easier to harvest and none is lost whilst the animal is grazing.

Sheep are well adapted to living on low quality herbage. They have four stomachs. Food passes into the first for temporary storage. Then, when the sheep finishes grazing, having filled this stomach, this food is returned to the mouth, a little at a time to be thoroughly chewed. Now called 'cud', this is swallowed again, passing on to the other three stomachs for complete digestion, extracting as much goodness as possible from each mouthful.

The intense artificial breeding means that some sheep breeds do better in certain environments than others. Some do best on scanty pasture, others require a rich herbage, some thrive in dry climates, some in wet, others need a warm habitat whilst yet others are admirably suited to the cold. Sheep breeds are incredibly variable. Even within a breed there are many strains. In the Welsh mountain breed there are over 24 different strains, each confined to a small locality, to which they are adapted, and each quite different from the others. Two examples are the Glamorgan and, a favourite of mine, the Beulah Speckled-face. As Thomas Peacock summed it up,

The mountain sheep are sweeter,
But the valley sheep are fatter;
We therefore deem it meeter
To carry off the latter.

In Wales and Britain generally, sheep are herded by dogs under the direction of a shepherd. Elsewhere, however, a man acts alone as the sheep's leader. This shepherd leads the sheep to pasture, and each animal is known by name and responds to being called. It is from this traditional way of life that the Christian religion takes its metaphor of Christ as Shepherd. Christ is also depicted as the Lamb of God. Long before Christ's time lambs were regarded as symbols of innocence, purity and righteousness. Rams were considered to epitomize strength and boldness. Indeed, in the time of the Pharaohs, sheep were held in such high regard that they were mummified and buried with these ancient kings. These sheep were kept purely for their wool, unlike those of the Israelites which were kept for their wool, milk and meat as well as for religious sacrifice.

In Britain sheep also have been of major importance, but this has been of an economic rather than a spiritual nature. Sheep naturally fertilized the ground and were an integral part of the rotation system of farming. Their wool was also for centuries a principal source of national revenue. So important that even today the Lord Chancellor's seat in the House of Lords is a large, square cushion stuffed with wool and known officially as the Woolsack.

Sadly, our attitude towards sheep is rather negative nowadays. We talk of someone as being a 'black sheep', a miscreant. In fact the saying comes from black sheep being unusual, the odd one out. A black lamb in a flock, however, used to be regarded as a good omen. We also talk, derogatively, of people 'following like sheep', perhaps you too can see that this is a twist on the truth. Yes, sheep follow, they follow a leader whom they can trust to do his best for them in finding food and shelter.

With our separation of animals from the preparation of our food, we tend to dismiss from our thoughts the fate of these creatures, which add so much delight to the countryside scene, not least here at Gilfach. Perhaps we should remember some of their qualities, they are extremely caring mothers, loyal to their home and leader; they are able to feel pain and are more intelligent than we give them credit. However, along with other domestic animals, they suffer extremely badly at the hands of man. Their welfare is of concern to many institutions especially in regard to the live transport of these creatures over hundreds of miles to slaughter houses in Britain and abroad. If we wish to exploit their meat and wool, we should grant them the basic rights of sentient beings.

BEULAH SPECKLE-FACED SHEEP.

7

HERE TODAY, GONE TOMORROW?

L ike a brooch set with precious stones, Gilfach decorates the mid-Wales landscape. A small but rare example of how this area once looked, a testimony to our heritage loss and an example of conservation in action.

We tend to think of conservation importance as referring to the need to save endangered species of one sort or another, and for many of us that means attractive mammals, exotic birds or colourful plants. Few of us feel instant empathy with the likes of snakes, millipedes or fungi. Yet these members of the world are just as essential a part of the web of life as the more glamorous species. The single oak leaf can feed a hundred gall wasp larvae which in turn provide a meal for small birds and bats, which themselves depend on other areas of Gilfach in which to live out part of their lifecycles. The small song birds and mammals are food for the predators, such as the buzzard. A breeding pair of these birds with two young require 100 kilogrammes (220 pounds) of meat a year. Roughly, this converts to 400 young rabbits or 3,300 voles.

The remains of dead animals provide food for all sorts of scavengers: crows and foxes as well as various insects such as ants and sexton beetles (*Silphidae*). The goodness from faeces, dead plant and animal tissues are returned to the ecosystem through the activities of these and others. Thanks to them, the plants, birds, animals, insects and fish can continue to play their own small, but vital, parts in the web of life.

Managers of conservation sites, such as Gilfach, need to be well versed in the intricacies of the ecological relationships. Conservation management is not as is easy as one might think. It is not a matter of leaving nature to its own devices and merely keeping the planners out. Conservation is really the art of preservation or, in some cases, re-creation. If a site like Gilfach was left to its own devices, succession would occur and over a short period of 50 -150 years the site would pass through a scrubby phase culminating in it being covered in woodland. But the conservation aims of such a site are to maintain species diversity, maintain the sites current basic status quo, preserve and, hopefully increase certain species, because they are rare and/or beautiful, and, finally, to preserve the 'naturalness' of the site – rather like a museum. I have put naturalness in inverted commas because much of what we see as our 'natural habitat' is the result of the various activities of man over many thousands of years.

WATER CROWFOOT.

153

For example, let us consider the grasslands of Gilfach, both in the meadows and on Wyloer Hill. As we have seen, these are the result of the underlying shales which were moulded during the ice ages and were once covered in woodland. Man, over the centuries removed that woodland, using the area mainly for grazing sheep. The plant communities resulting from these centuries of grazing are what we now consider as the 'natural, unspoilt' landscape of mid-Wales we so enjoy.

It is the aim of the Radnorshire Wildlife Trust to conserve and enhance this landscape both for our enjoyment and for the benefit of the species within it. To do this, the grassland cannot be allowed to revert to successive stages of scrub and eventual woodland. The sward must be kept. This could be achieved by several methods: the area could be burnt annually, mown mechanically or grazed. Burning has intrinsic problems, partly because the area is wet and also because of controlling fires so they do not spread. Not least, burning is damaging to the insects and creatures who rely on insects for their own food. Many insects cannot escape the flames. Though some can fly and others bury themselves underground, populations of other species would be devastated if fire was used as a conservation tool here. In other areas, such as parts of the New Forest, controlled burning is an appropriate conservation tool. Mowing and burning have another disadvantage, they are both indiscriminate. The time at which an area is mown or burnt may be correct for some plant species in the sward yet stop others from completing their annual reproduction cycles. Having said that, mowing is a useful measure when, for example, hay meadows are being conserved, though the timing is critical.

For Gilfach's conservation sheep grazing has many advantages. Sheep are selective feeders who eat by nibbling plant tops. They do not destroy the growing point of the plant, nor do they eat all members of the population in one go. Indeed they often only eat certain parts of plants. Whilst food goes in one end, it emerges from the other in the form of dung which serves to fertilize the soil, thereby enriching the growth of plants. While cattle and horses also provide dung, they are heavy animals and their weight causes their hooves to break the turf turning the ground into a mudbath. In contrast, the sheep's light weight and dainty, pointed feet merely break up the dead plant matter on the surface, allowing light, air and moisture to reach new growth and even buried seeds underneath. Sheep are basically grass eaters and at low densities will leave many of the flowering plants alone, which in turn provide nectar for insects, who provide food for small birds and mammals who in turn are food for others. Gilfach is lightly stocked with sheep who graze the upper slopes throughout the year and are rotated through the meadows to the best advantage of the plants found there.

The sheep are not allowed to graze throughout Gilfach. In the interests of conservation, they are excluded from the wood, allowing the ground flora and understorey to generate and flourish, including seedling oaks. They are also excluded from parts of the riverbank to ensure that bankside vegetation is not damaged, nor the banks' structure threatened. The otter is a creature whose population is threatened throughout Britain, mainly through loss of suitable habitat. Gilfach is important to the local otter population as it is a waterway linking the Severn and Wye rivers. Making the Marteg a more attractive habitat to otters will enable the population to increase and spread. Excluding sheep and humans from stretches of the bank will provide a variety of undisturbed habitats in which these timid creatures can lie up, frolic and rear their young. Whilst the banks can be maintained and enhanced to attract creatures such as kingfisher, heron and otter, conservation of the river itself is more tricky. It is difficult to control the water purity; pollution, be it from accidental spillages upriver or from the cumulative effects of pesticides and fertilizers, is not under the control of the Trust.

Although Gilfach does contain some rare species, such as the mountain pansy, the upright vetch and its lichens, its conservation importance lies in the way it typefies the natural landscape of the area. Such 'typical' areas which are now increasingly threatened.

Sadly, even here in beautiful mid-Wales, it is a truism to say that all that grows is not 'green'. Vast tracts of the British landscape have been changed radically over the last few decades. The statistics make depressing reading. Since the late 1940s, 95% of our flower-rich hay meadows have disappeared because the pastures and hillsides have been 'improved' with fertilizers and pesticides. Re-seeded with one or two grass species, they contrast starkly with the variety of life, flora and fauna supported by traditional hay meadows. Fifty per cent of our ancient woodland has been lost forever: not just the trees, but the plants and animals as well. Even primroses and bluebells are becoming scarce in the wild. The uplands are being drained for forestry plantations or for improved pasture land. The draining destroys the habitat for specialist species and the so-called common cotton grass which, like so many other 'common' species, is no longer common at all. Between 1945 and 1985, 96,000 miles (153,600 kilometres) of hedgerow were uprooted and in the following 5 years to 1990 a further 53,000 miles (84,800 kilometres) were annihilated. Our rivers too have suffered. Farmers and foresters have straightened the banks and cleared them of vegetation thereby eliminating rich habitats. River water has been extracted for human use without due consideration of nature's needs. Man's hunger for water has also destroyed vast tracts of land through flooding, such as in nearby Elan. Many rivers and ponds and lakes are polluted, not just by industrial waste but by individuals who seem to think that a body of water is a dustbin in which to dump old prams, cars, and other rubbish.

All this has destroyed ecosystems which had developed over millennia. What was typical has rapidly become rare. Hence the basic importance and attraction of Gilfach, which has not undergone any major transformations for hundreds of years, and this is reflected in its flora and fauna. As has been illustrated in the preceding chapters, Gilfach contains many plant species ranging from mighty oaks to tiny velvet-like lichens and fungi, has an upland bird community worthy of note, provides a major waterway for otters and a much needed winter home for a number of bat species. It is for reasons such as these that Gilfach has gained the status of a Site of Special Scientific Interest (SSSI), a recognition which affords *no* legal protection.

Whilst the promise for the well-being of Gilfach lies in its acquisition and its future management by the members of the Radnorshire Wildlife Trust, their success can only occur if the site is protected from pollution and compulsory purchase. It is for each of us do our part to ensure the health of our own small piece of the planet by considering how our own lifestyle impinges on nature and by attempting to ensure our natural heritage is legally protected. Charity and conservation both begin at home.

MARSH MARIGOLD.

INDEX

agaric 139
alder 21, 22, 57, 95, 120, 122
alder kitten 111
algae 72, 108, 110
ants 128, 137, 138, 146, 153
aphids 128, 138
ash 13, 22, 24, 34, 56, 57, 91, 107, 110, 120, 132
aspen 22

badger 128, 135, 136, 137
balsa 90
banks 41, 109, 116, 120, 121, 122, 155, 156
bark 22, 23, 24, 58, 59, 62, 65, 68, 69, 70, 71, 72, 78, 93, 96, 128
barn owl 76
bat 12, 23, 42, 44, 45, 48, 49, 50, 52, 53, 64, 76, 77, 85, 95, 111, 112, 113, 116, 117, 120, 129, 153, 154, 156
bedstraw 135
beech 57
beetle 78, 146
betony 125
bilberry 88, 147
birch 21, 22, 57, 61, 95, 97, 120, 122
bird's foot trefoil 141
biting midge 72
bitter vetch 121
bluebell 84, 141, 155
bog asphodel 122
boulder 15, 17, 103, 109, 120, 121
Brachythecium rivulare 110
bracken 142, 144, 146
bramble 84, 128
bramble gall wasp 128
Bronze Age 25, 26
brown bent 145
brown long-eared 44, 52, 53, 85
bugle 125
bullhead 112, 113, 116
bumble bee 128
bundling 40
burnet saxifrage 37, 69
burrow 52, 135

buttercup 121
butterwort 122, 147
buzzard 38, 85, 133, 135, 148, 153

caddis fly 53, 109, 120
canopy 64, 66, 84, 85, 90, 96
carnivores 80, 112, 116
carr 122
Carroll 139
caterpillar 139, 142
chaffinch 96
climax 61, 62
coal-tit 96
common cotton-grass 146
common shrew 130
common toadflax 128
common treecreeper 85
conservation 12, 31, 76, 153, 154, 155, 156
coppicing 23, 71
crows 38, 135, 153
cruck 33, 34
Culpeper 141
current 99, 104, 107, 108, 109, 110, 111, 114, 118, 153
Cyclops 72

damselflies 108, 120
dandelion 62, 121
dark green fritillary 142
Daubenton 53
decomposition 77, 84, 85, 90, 138, 146
deforestation 95
dendro-chronology 60
detritivores 77, 83, 97, 138
devil's bit scabious 141
devil's coach horse 78
Devonian 14
dipper 119
ditches 97, 124, 135
dog rose 128
dog violet 142
domestication 149
dragonflies 53, 108, 119, 120

Druid 60
Dunkeld larch 88
Dutch Elm Disease 76
dyer's greenwood 141

earthworm 78, 136
ecosystem 62, 64, 77, 84, 104, 112, 114, 153, 156
elm 21, 24, 76
erosion 23, 103, 107
eyebright 125

farming 24, 26, 27, 28, 31, 34, 36, 138, 144, 150
fertilizer 134
Ffrwd Fawr 103, 104, 113, 114, 121
fields 24, 25, 37, 50, 84, 124, 133, 134, 135, 148
Fissidens rufulus 121
flax 41, 128
flushes 134
Forestry Commission 88, 96
forget-me-not 110
fossil 13, 15, 90
foxglove 125
frog 115, 116, 135
Fuccidea recensa 147

gall wasp 66, 128, 153
galls 65, 66
Galoplaca sudpallida 147
Gamallt 41, 88, 92, 93, 96, 97, 100, 142
gamekeeper 82
giant puffball 139
glacier 14, 15, 16, 17, 18, 57
globeflower 121
goldcrest 76, 96, 98
goldfinch 132, 142
goosander 114
goose-grass 125
gorse 88
goshawk 96, 97, 133
grasshopper 128
grayling 112, 113, 114, 117

greater spotted woodpecker 85
green oak moth 52, 66
green-veined white 142
grey wagtail 120

habitat 12, 23, 25, 41, 42, 50, 53, 56, 64, 70, 72, 76, 77, 78, 82, 85, 93, 97, 98, 102, 107, 108, 110, 116, 117, 120, 121, 124, 134, 137, 146, 149, 153, 155, 156
Haematomma ventuosum 148
harebell 141
hawkweed 121
hawthorn 22, 97, 128, 142
hay 12, 28, 29, 32, 36, 37, 102, 124, 134, 140, 142, 145, 147, 154, 155
hazel 21, 22, 23, 61
hedge 124, 125, 128, 129, 130, 132, 133, 142, 145, 149
hedge-sparrow 128
hedgehog 82, 85, 128, 129, 130
hedgerow 12, 50, 82, 96, 124, 128, 132, 135, 142, 155
hedges 82, 84, 124, 125, 136
herb layer 84, 85
herbivores 24, 80, 133
heron 115, 116, 117, 135, 155
hibernaculum 44, 45, 49, 53
holly 22, 60, 84
honey fungus 64
honeysuckle 121
horse chestnut 57
horse mushroom 139
hoverfly 72
Hyocomium armoricum 121
Hywel Dda 26, 27, 28

insectivores 50
interglacial 15, 18
Iron Age 26
Isothecium holtii 121

Jack-by-the-hedge 142
jackdaw 96
jay 62, 63, 96

kestrel 76
kingfisher 115, 155
kite 38, 133, 135

ladybird 76
Lammas 67

Lejeunea lamacerina 121
lesser skullcap 121
lesser spearwort 110
lesser spotted woodpecker 85
Leucobryum juniperoideum 121
light chimney 64, 84
lime 20, 24, 65, 108, 119, 134
ling heather 88
liverwort 69, 121
lodgepole 88, 92
longhouse 12, 31, 32, 33, 34, 37
lousewort 134, 135

magpie 96
management 64, 92, 100, 153, 156
marsh bedstraw 135
marsh marigold 122
marsh pennywort 135
marsh St John's wort 135
marsh tit 111
Marteg 12, 16, 17, 31, 36, 41, 53, 97, 102, 103, 104, 106, 107, 110, 112, 113, 114, 116, 117, 119, 120, 121, 122, 135, 147, 155
mat grass 145
mayflies 108, 113, 119, 120
medicine 93, 125
Mesolithic 22, 23
milk cap 41
minotaur beetle 146
mint 110, 122
mole 82, 138, 146
Monk's Trod 24, 28, 29
moraine 17
mosquito 72, 107, 120
mountain ash 22
mountain pansy 141, 155
Murchison 13
myxomatosis 82, 133, 136

natterer 42, 44
navelwort 131
Neolithic 23, 24, 25, 56, 88, 149
nest box 76, 99, 132
nettle 52
niche 85, 93, 112
nightingale 74
non-biting midge 72
Norway spruce 92
nuthatch 128

oakwood 12, 56, 57, 61, 62, 64, 65, 85, 88, 91, 93, 95, 96, 124, 128, 142, 148
oligotrophic 110
orange elf-cup 41
orbweb spider 128
Ordovician 13
Orthopodomyia pulchripalpis 72
otter 116, 117, 118, 119, 135, 155, 156
oxygen 68, 104, 107, 111, 112, 113

paramecium 72
parasol mushroom 139
parrot fungus 140
Peacock, Thomas, 149
pedunculate oak 22, 57
penny bun fungus 97
perch 112
pesticides 52, 133, 134, 155
photosynthesis 68
pied flycatcher 76
pike 112
pipistrelle 44, 45, 49, 52, 53
plankton 107
plantation 12, 56, 88, 90, 93, 96, 142, 148, 155
podzol 21
polecat 81, 82, 83, 84, 85, 135, 136
pollard 73
pollen 21, 22
pollutants 69
pollution 19, 50, 68, 69, 116, 117, 155, 156
primrose 84, 122, 155
Prionocyphon serricornis 72
puffball 139
purple moor grass 37, 145

rabbit 58, 63, 78, 81, 82, 133, 135, 136, 138, 146, 147, 153
Radnorshire Wildlife Trust 12, 31, 97, 142, 154, 156
ragged robin 37
ragwort 41
railway 12, 29, 31, 41, 45, 92, 97, 122, 148
rain shadow 15
recycling 77
red oak roller weevil 65
redpoll 95
Rhayader 12, 28, 29, 36, 102, 147

ribwort plantain 141
ringlet 142
robin 37, 76, 96
rush 134
rushlights 36, 134
rye-grass 134

salmon 104, 112, 114, 115, 117
Scots pine 21, 29
sessile oak 21, 22, 56, 57, 62, 97
shale 12, 13, 154
sheep 24, 25, 26, 28, 29, 34, 36, 37, 38, 40, 41, 56, 58, 63, 81, 84, 93, 121, 122, 124, 125, 133, 134, 135, 144, 145, 146, 149, 150, 154, 155
sheep's fescue 145
sheep lice 134
shrub layer 90
Silurian 13, 14
siskin 90, 95, 96, 98
sitka spruce 88, 92
skylark 147, 148
small heath 142
small skipper 142
small toadflax 41, 128
snail 76
soft-rush 134
soil 12, 18, 19, 20, 21, 23, 24, 25, 26, 56, 57, 62, 63, 64, 65, 66, 67, 69, 78, 80, 85, 90, 104, 116, 121, 122, 136, 147, 149, 154, 156, 157
spaghnum 147
sparrowhawk 96, 97

springtails 80
squirrel 56, 62, 63, 64, 76, 85, 88, 90
SSSI 156
St John's wort 125, 135
stag beetle 78
stone loach 111, 112, 113
stoneflies 108
sundew 122, 147
sweet chestnut 57
Swift 119
sycamore 57, 62

tannin 68, 72, 93
tawny owl 76
thistle 133, 142
thrush 74
tit 76, 96, 128
Tolpuddle 66
trout 112, 113, 114, 117
tunnel 12, 41, 42, 44, 45, 53, 65, 78, 138
turnip moth 52

Umbilicaria deusta 147
understorey 84, 155
unimproved 134, 140, 146

walls 12, 16, 19, 25, 33, 44, 58, 69, 124, 135
water crowfoot 97
water pepper 110
water shrimp 108
wavy bittercress 97

wavy hair-grass 145
weasel 81, 135
weevil 65
whiskered 44, 49, 53
wildwood 22, 23, 24, 25
willow 22, 97, 110, 136
willow moss 110
willowherb 97
winter moth 66
wolf spider 80
wood anemone 84
wood warbler 85
woodland 22, 25, 26, 53, 56, 61, 62, 63, 64, 69, 76, 77, 82, 84, 85, 97, 98, 120, 122, 124, 153, 154, 155
woodlice 76, 78, 80
woodmouse 63, 76, 81, 84, 128, 136
woodpecker 71, 85
wool 28, 29, 40, 41, 134, 147, 149, 150
Woolsack 150
wren 119, 128, 132
Wye 12, 13, 16, 17, 41, 102, 103, 114, 155
Wyloer 12, 18, 24, 34, 41, 63, 124, 142, 145, 146, 147, 148, 154

yellow cow-wheat 121
yellow flag 135, 141
yellow meadow ant 137
yellow rattle 37
yew 29, 90